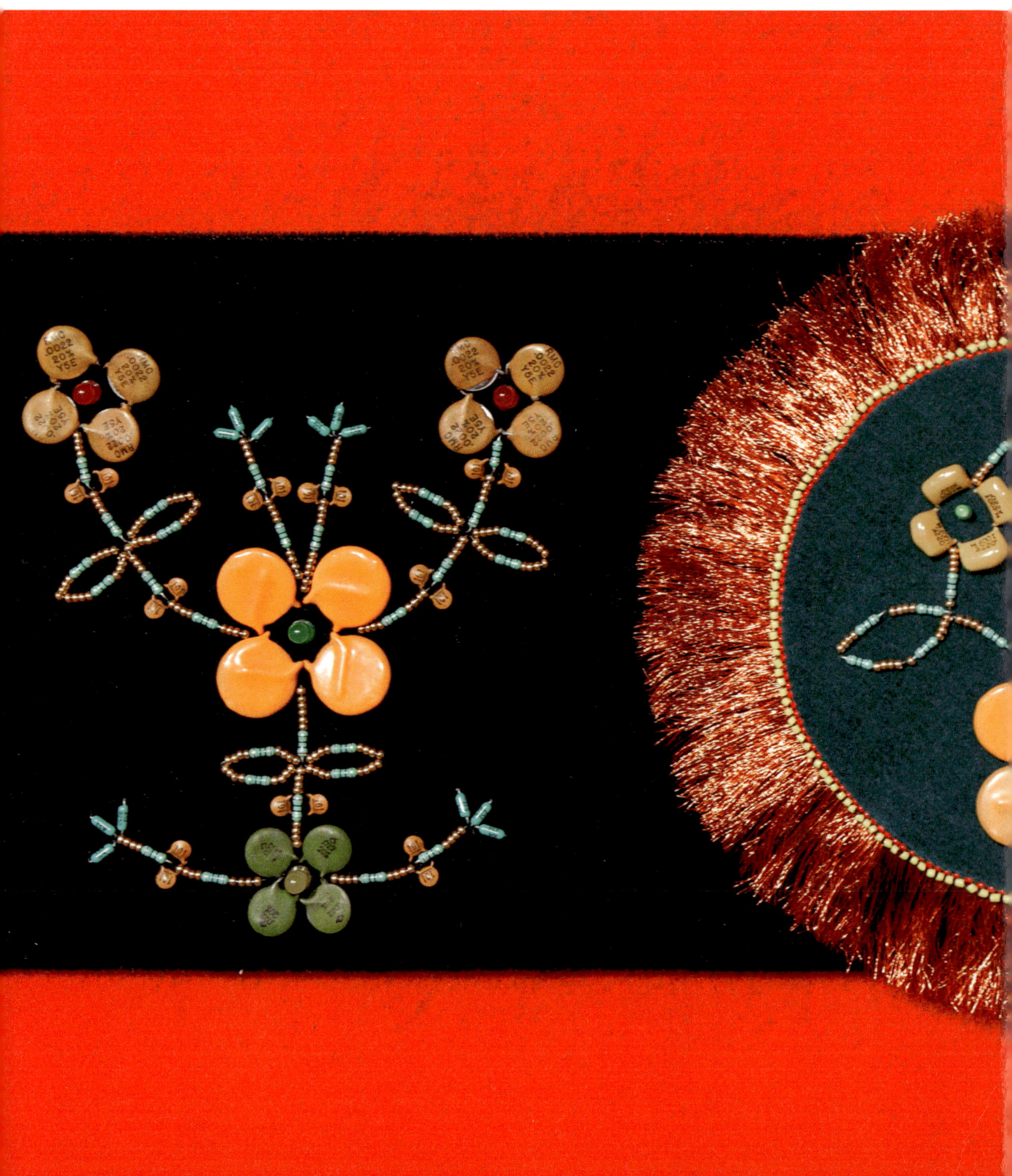

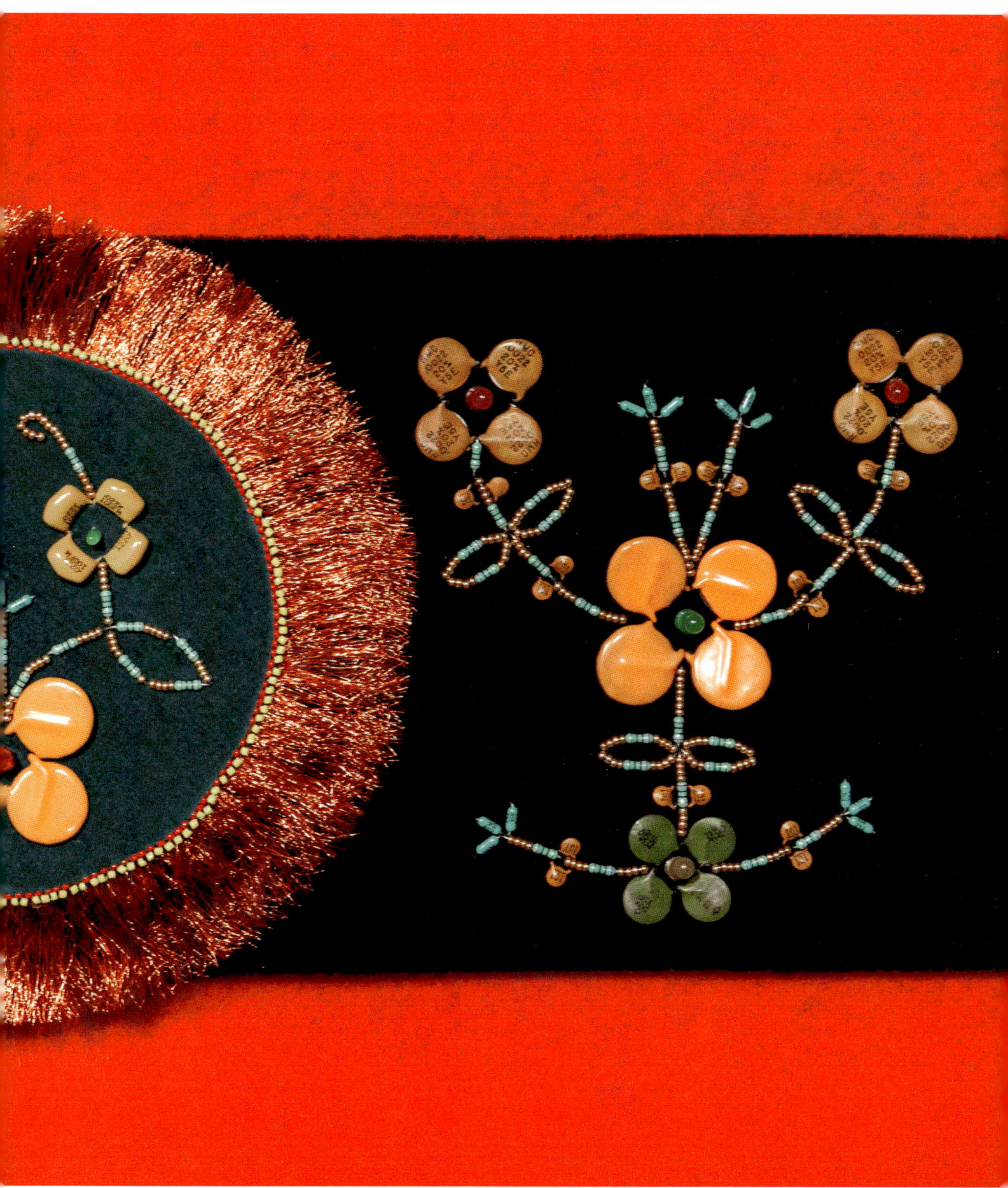

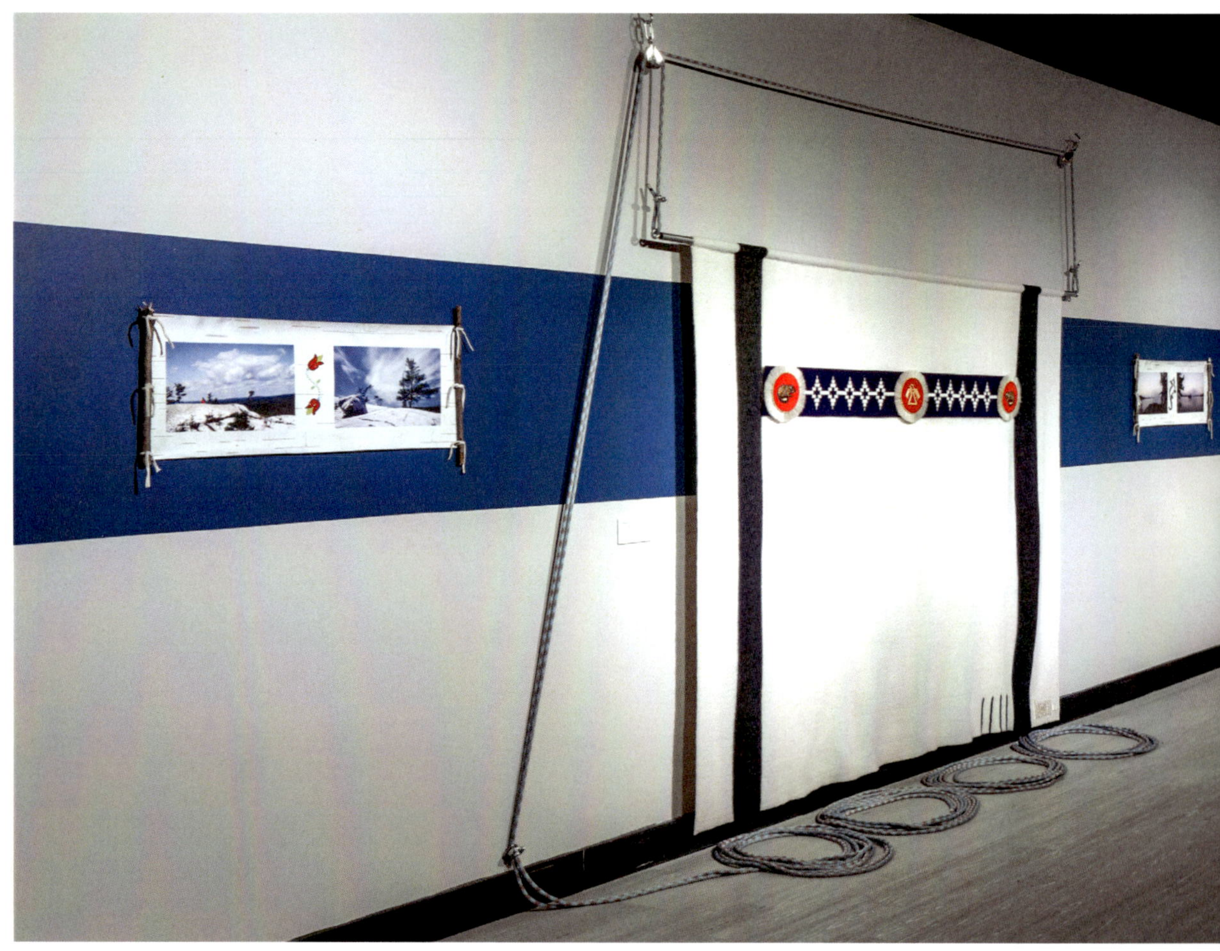

Gichi-zaaga'igan Lake Ontario (Big Lake), Detail, 2016, Hudson Bay blanket, velvet, beads, transistors, horse hair, metal, mountain climbing rope.
COLLECTION OF THE ARTIST

Aanikegamaa-gichigami: Lake Erie (Chain of Lakes Sea), 2016, Hudson Bay blanket, velvet, beads, electronic components, metal, mountain climbing rope.
COLLECTION OF THE ARTIST

Gichi-aazhoogami-gichigami: Lake Huron (Great Crosswaters Sea), 2016, Hudson Bay blanket, velvet, beads, transistors, horse hair, metal, mountain climbing rope. COLLECTION OF THE ARTIST

Memory Landscape, (select précis of 30), 2014, Digital output on archival canvas, glass beads, wood, hide.
COLLECTION OF THE ARTIST

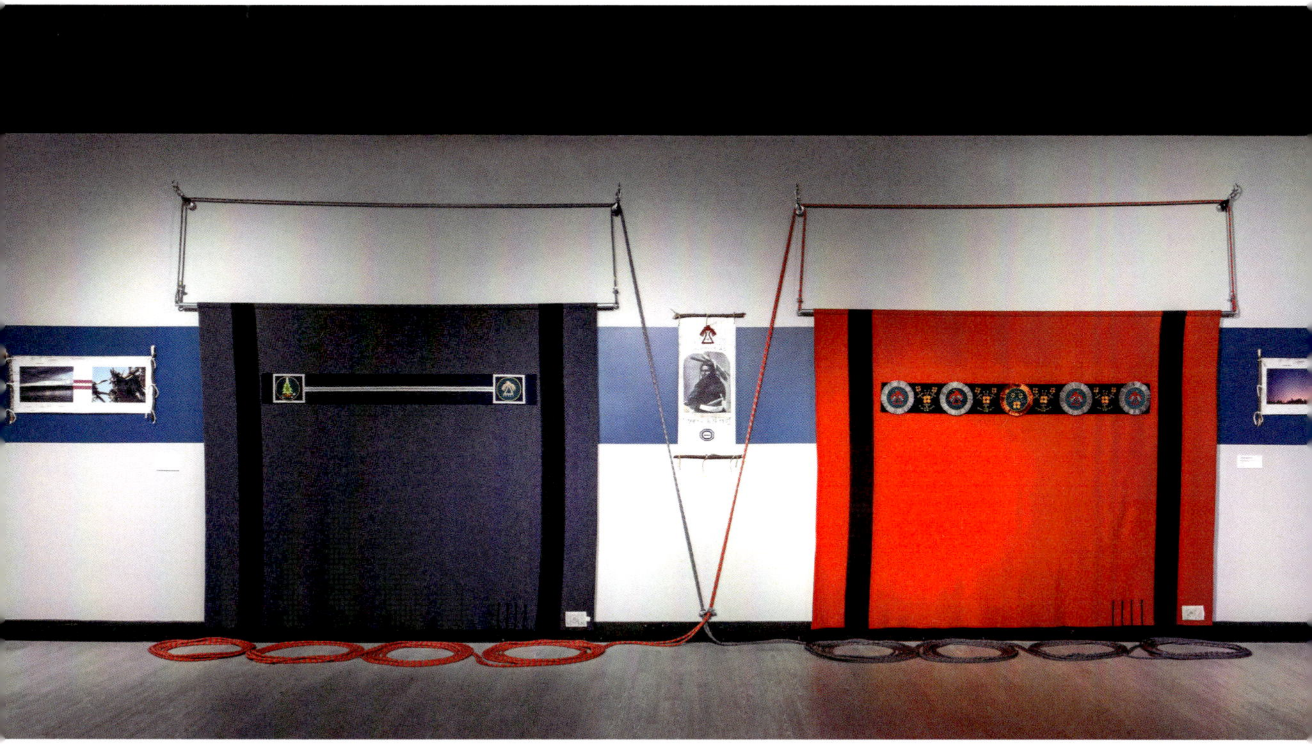

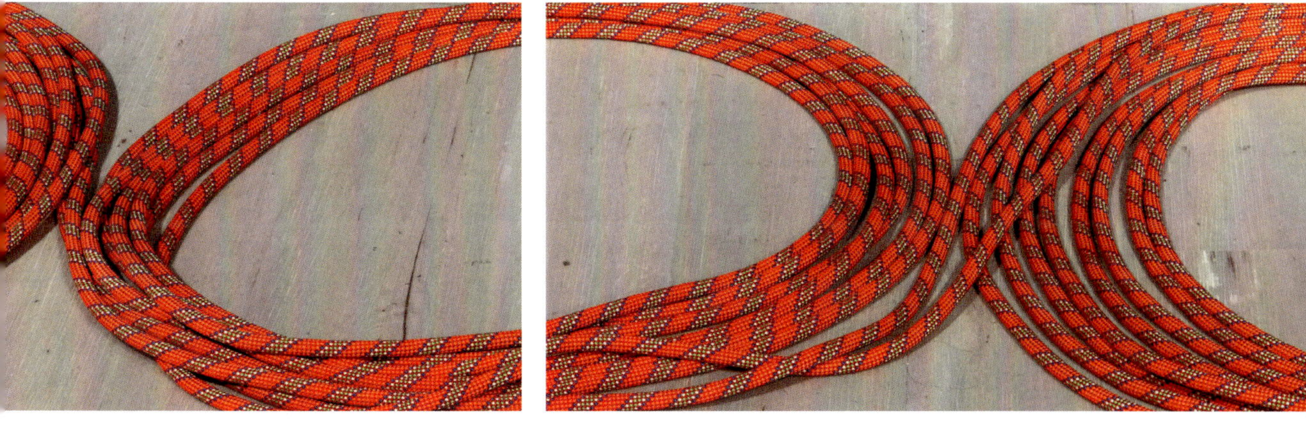

There is never an easy or straightforward way in honouring one's heritage. Ultimately you strive to share a narrative that will impart knowledge, express the uniqueness of your cultural identity, and recognize the generational traditions that have helped to formulate who you have become. These characteristics are definitely reflected in the eloquence and beauty of Barry Ace's work.

My introduction to Barry's work came in 2016 when I discovered *Baby Warrior*, a digital print representing a vintage baby doll with Anishinaabeg floral motifs as its clothing. I was immediately drawn to the image. The playfulness and the innocence disguised within the inner struggle of Indigenous cultural identity piqued my curiosity. It also triggered questions within me on the process of reclaiming cultural identity and how we can change the lens in which we see others. This ultimately led me to Ace and the development of his *Coalesce* exhibition and this accompanying catalogue.

Coalesce highlights mixed-media works that continue Ace's exploration into the reconstruction of identity through art. In Ace's work, the historical and the contemporary converge; distinct Anishinaabeg aesthetics of the Great Lakes region fuse with Western society's materials and technology, as revealed in the intricate floral and geometric Anishinaabeg beadwork that merges traditional glass-cut beads and natural fibres with reclaimed electronic circuitry. This intentional entanglement of materials shifts our paradigm of thinking and challenges us to re-examine notions of cultural stasis.

In addition to cultural borderlands, Ace's work takes us on journeys through geographical, spatial, and temporal dimensions. His Anishinaabeg honour blankets—*Gichi-zaaga'igan, Lake Ontario; Gichi-aazhoogami-gichigami, Lake Huron;* and *Aanikegamaa-gichigami, Lake Erie*—represent the traditional territory on which the Gallery resides. The endearing *Memory Landscape* scrolls commemorate Ace's adopted brother and his passing into the spirit world. The final work in the exhibition, the impressive *Bandoliers for Aki, Nibi, Noodin* features beadwork combined with LED readouts of the words "Land," "Water," and "Wind," and abstract symbols of each. These works reinforce the importance of acknowledging Indigenous cultural continuity, past, present, and future.

On behalf of the Robert Langen Art Gallery, I would like to sincerely thank Canadian scholar, filmmaker, and writer Armand Garnet Ruffo for providing a literary piece inspired by the works in the exhibition. Through Ruffo's historical voyage, our eyes are opened to the evolution and reinvention of Indigenous art-making.

A special thank you to the Office of Indigenous Initiatives at Wilfrid Laurier University and the Laurier Library for their generous financial assistance in supporting this publication. Thanks also go to WLU Press for helping to spearhead the execution of the catalogue, and to Betty Winge for designing a publication that embraces our vision.

Lastly, I extend my deepest gratitude to Barry Ace for his continued dedication and enthusiasm for this exhibition and publication. His creative insight, collaborative spirit, and willingness to mentor our Laurier students during his campus visits truly made this project a rewarding experience. Drawing from his own personal family experience and that of the Anishinaabeg community, Ace's storytelling leaves us with new ways of seeing and appreciating each other.

Suzanne Luke
Curator
Robert Langen Art Gallery

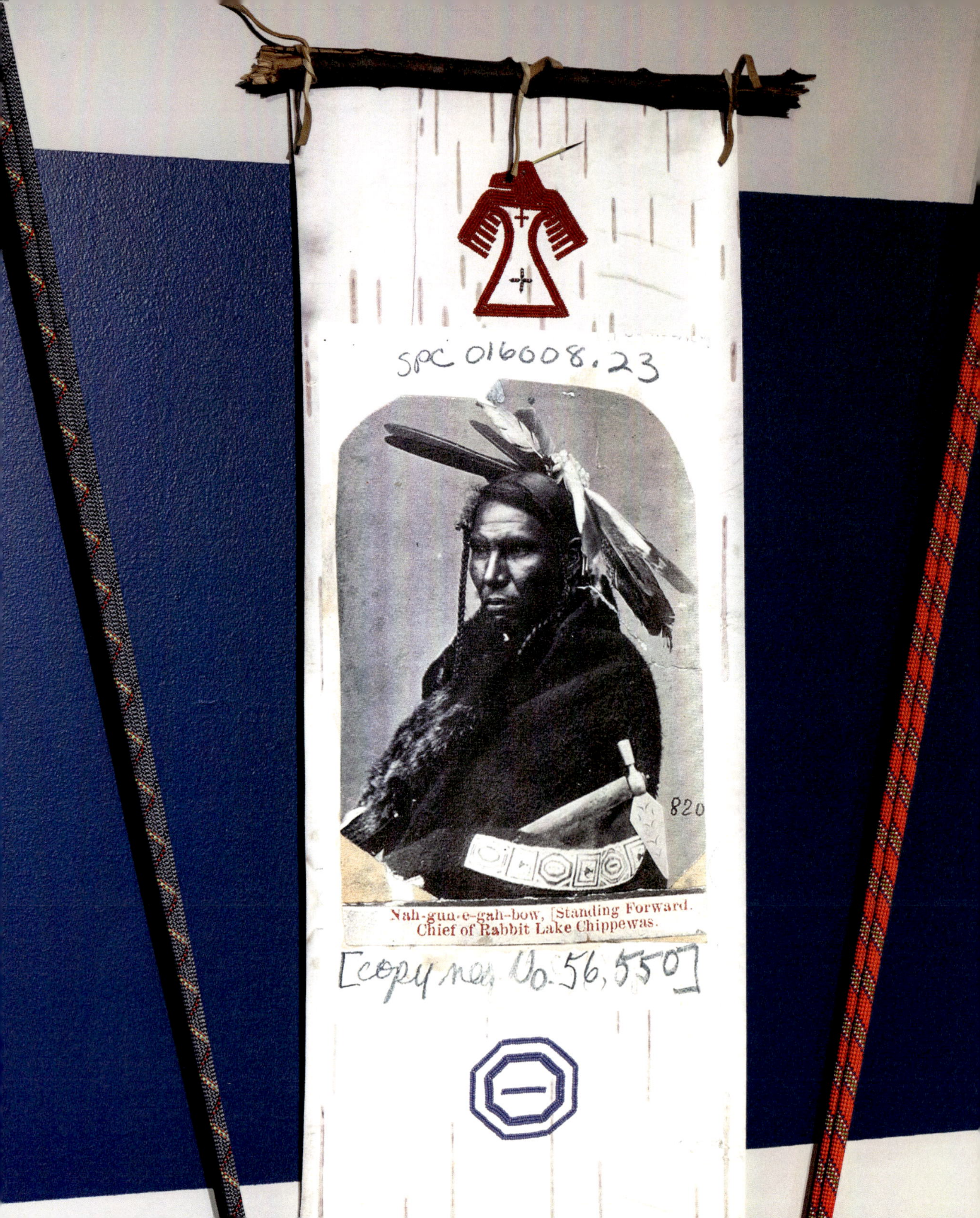
SPC 016008.23
820
Nah-gun-e-gah-bow, [Standing Forward.
Chief of Rabbit Lake Chippewas.
[copy neg. no.56,550]

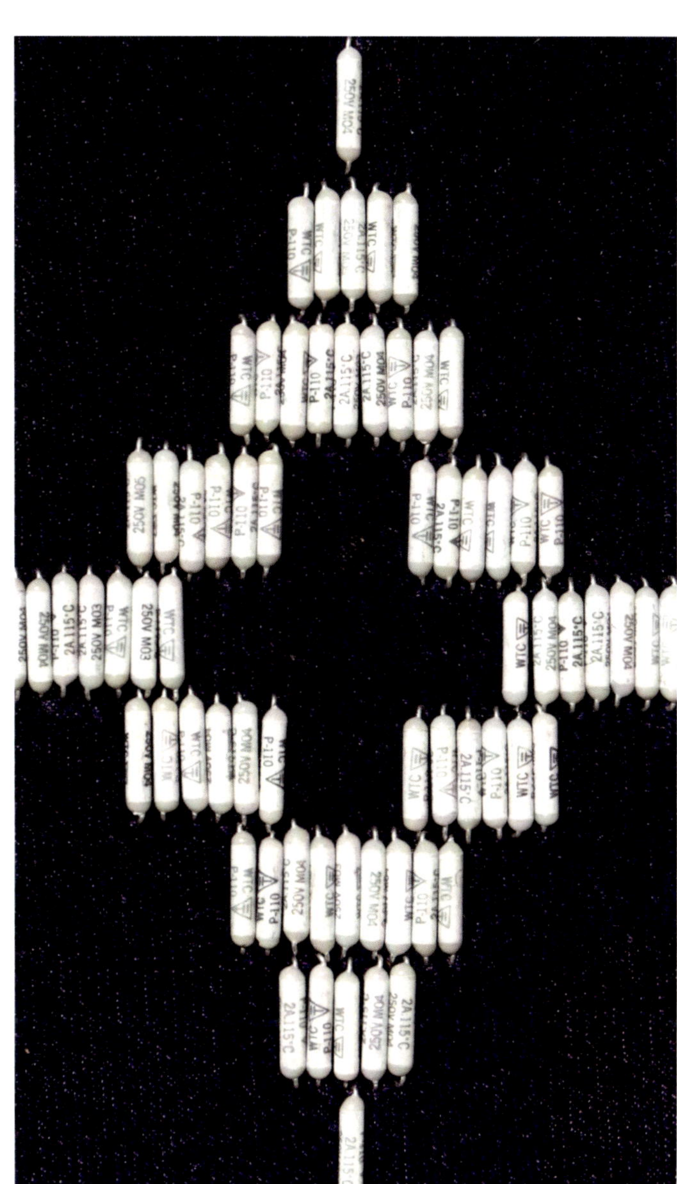

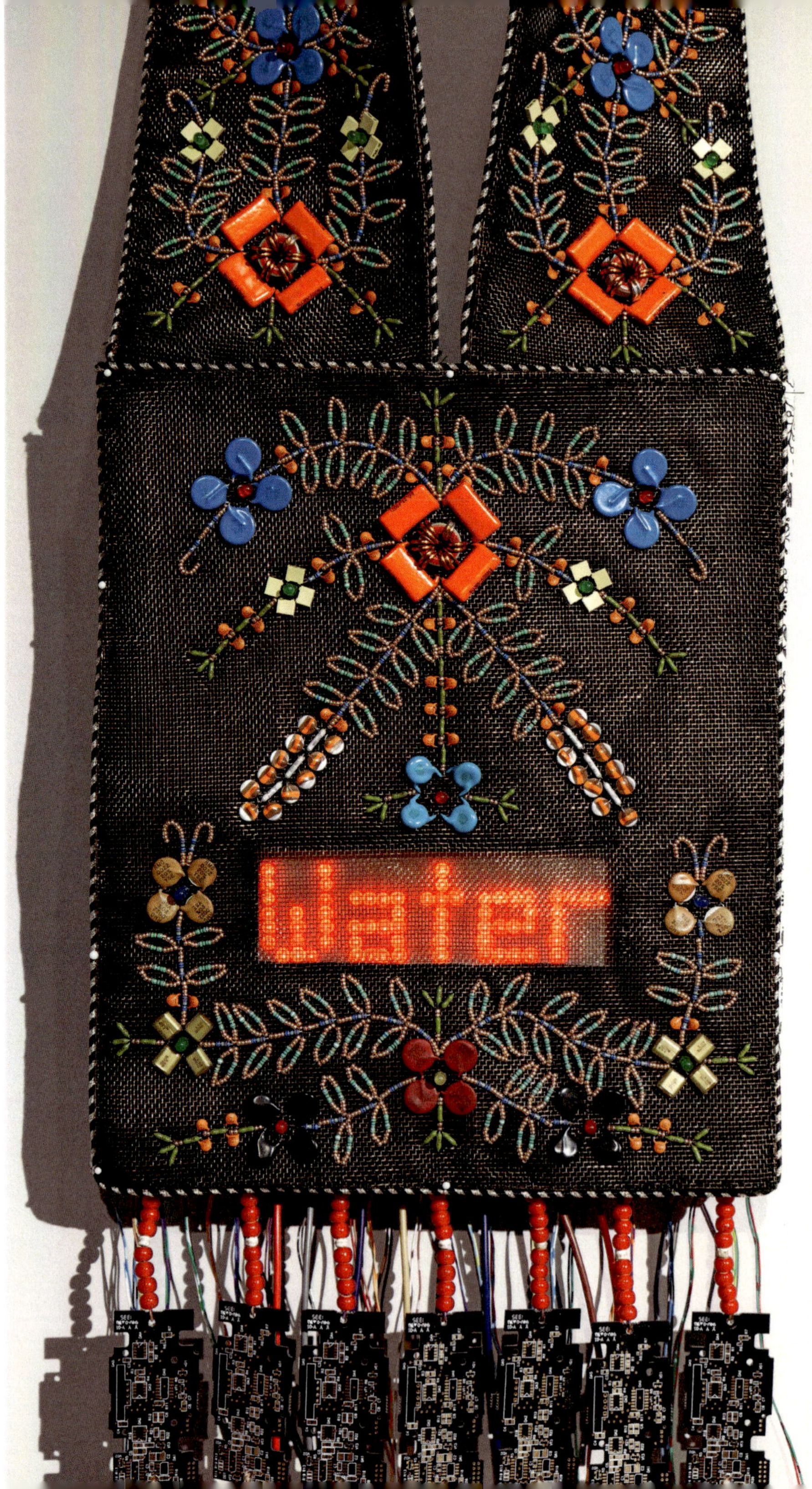
water

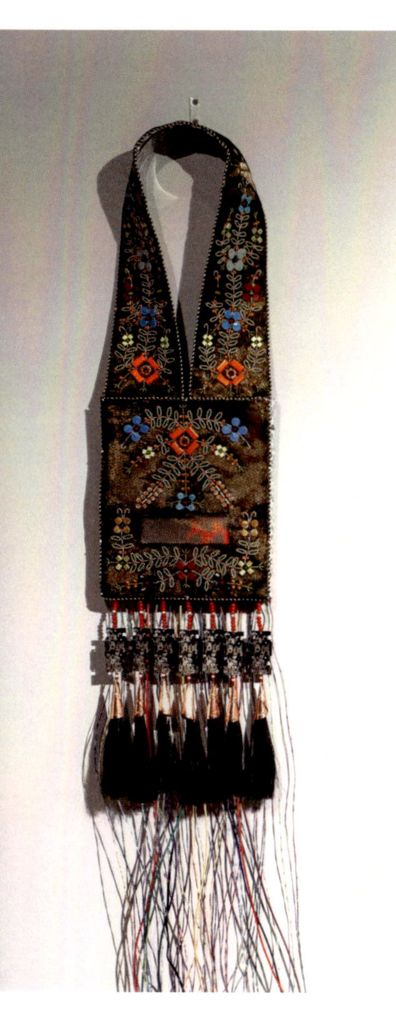 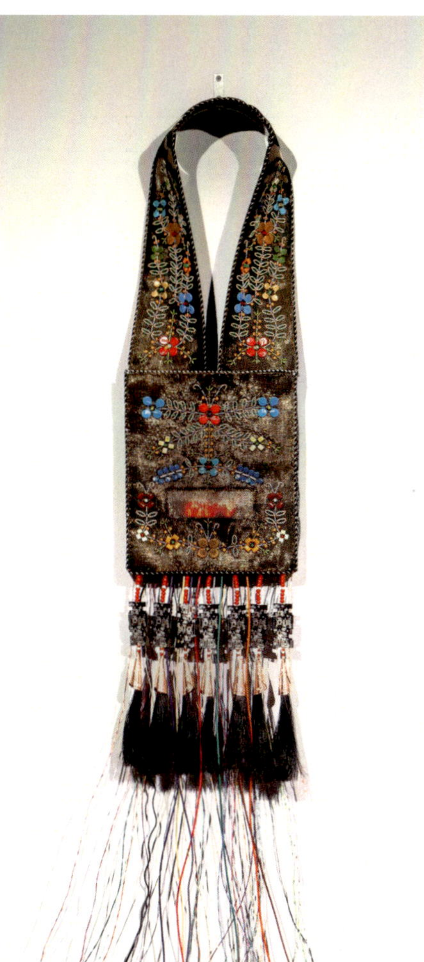 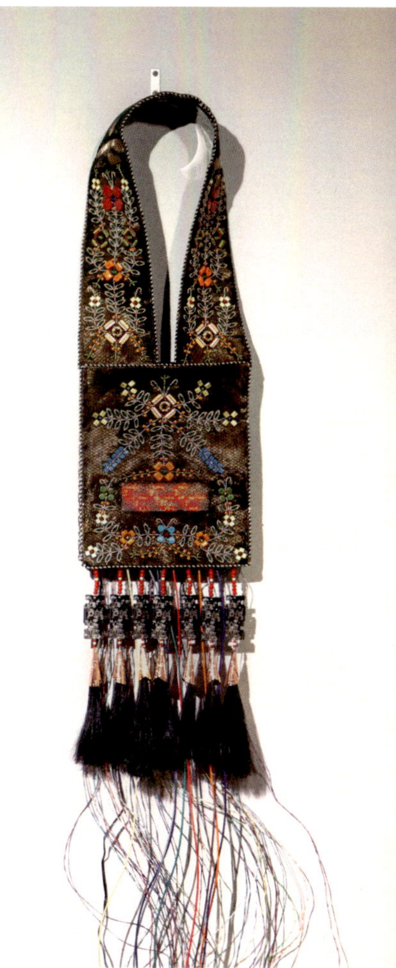

Bandoliers for Aki, Nibi, Noodin, 2019, Bronze screen, velvet,
electronic components, LED scrolling messenger devices, metal,
paper, plastic, metal, copper, calico, synthetic material.
COLLECTION OF THE ARTIST

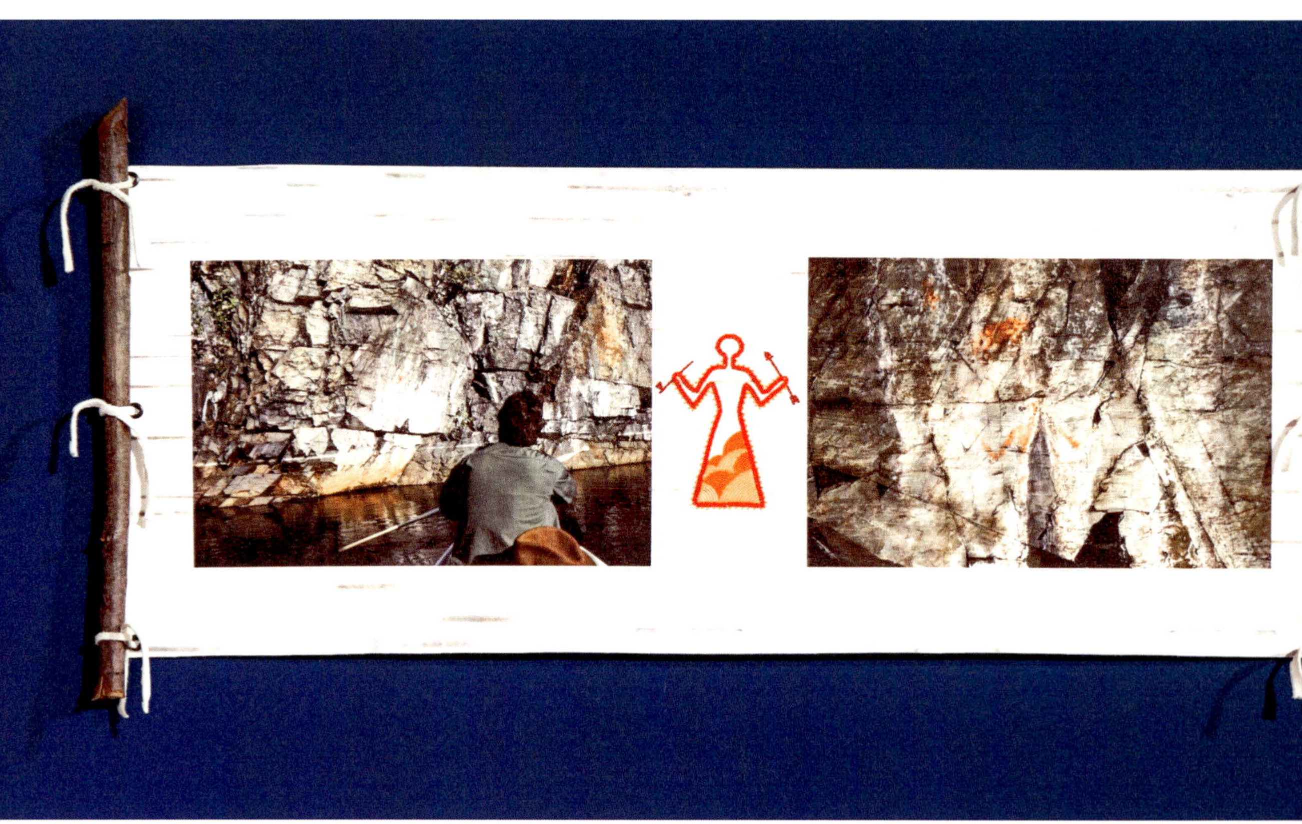

Memory Landscape, (select précis of 30), 2014, Detail
digital output on archival canvas, glass beads, wood, hide.

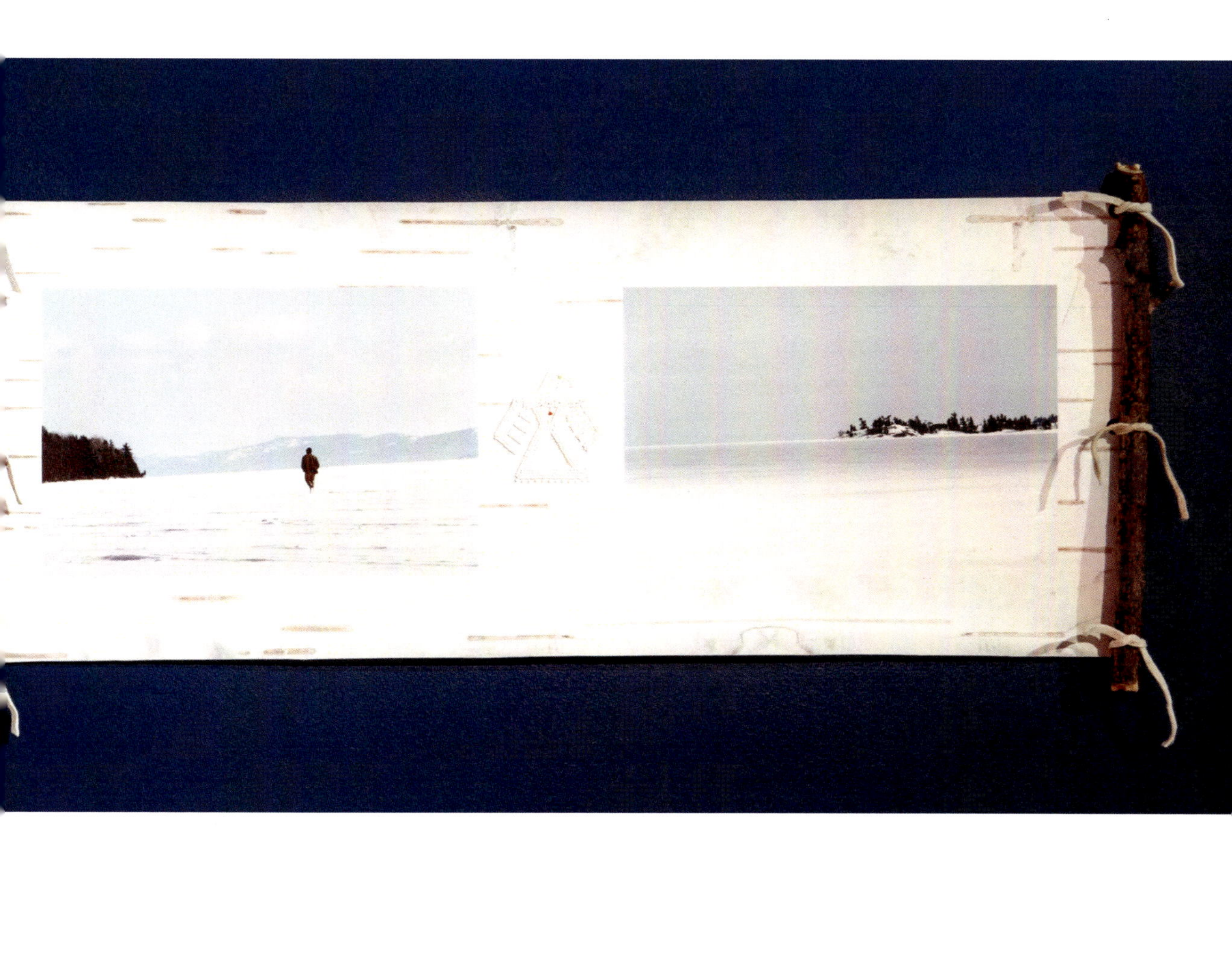

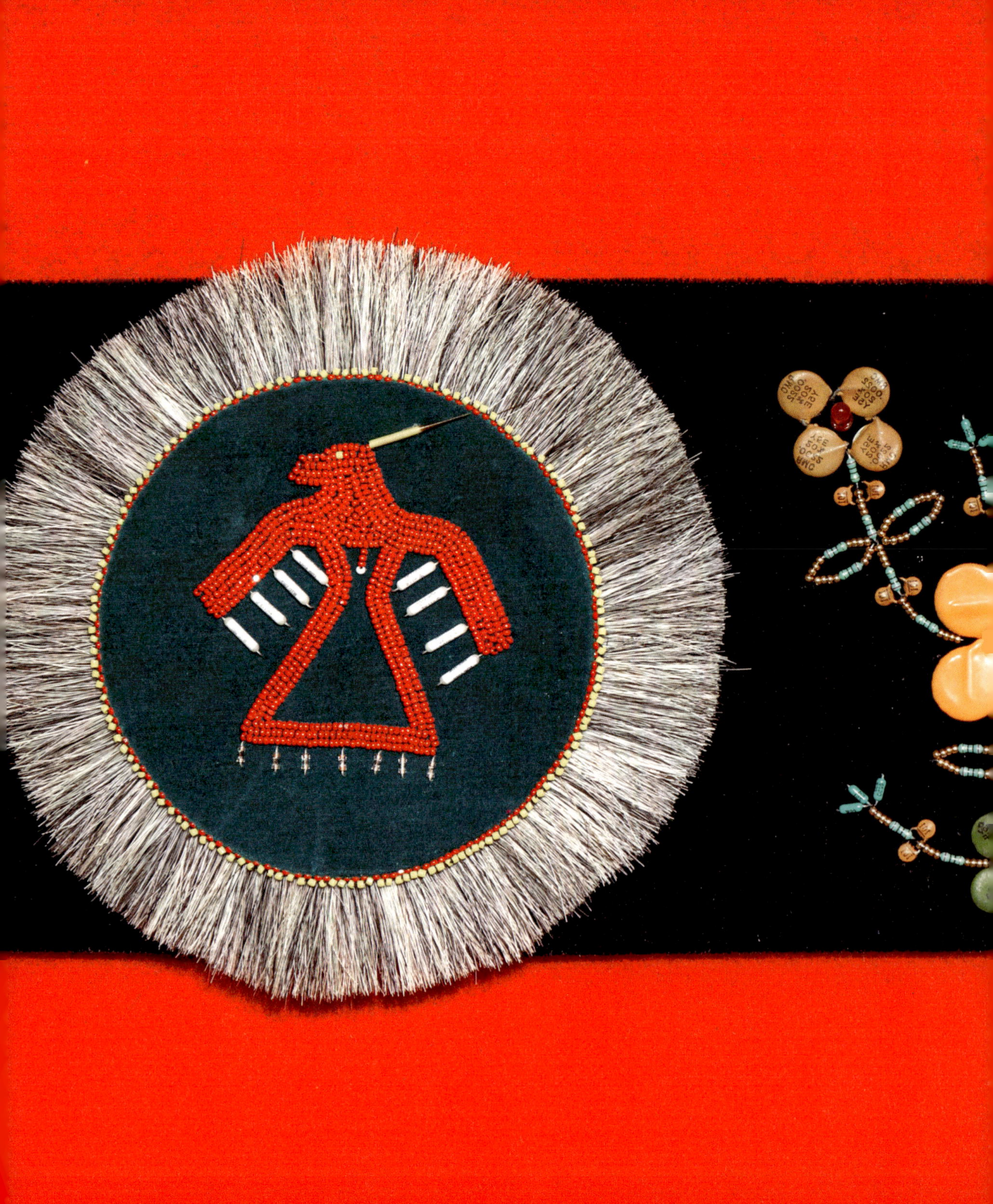

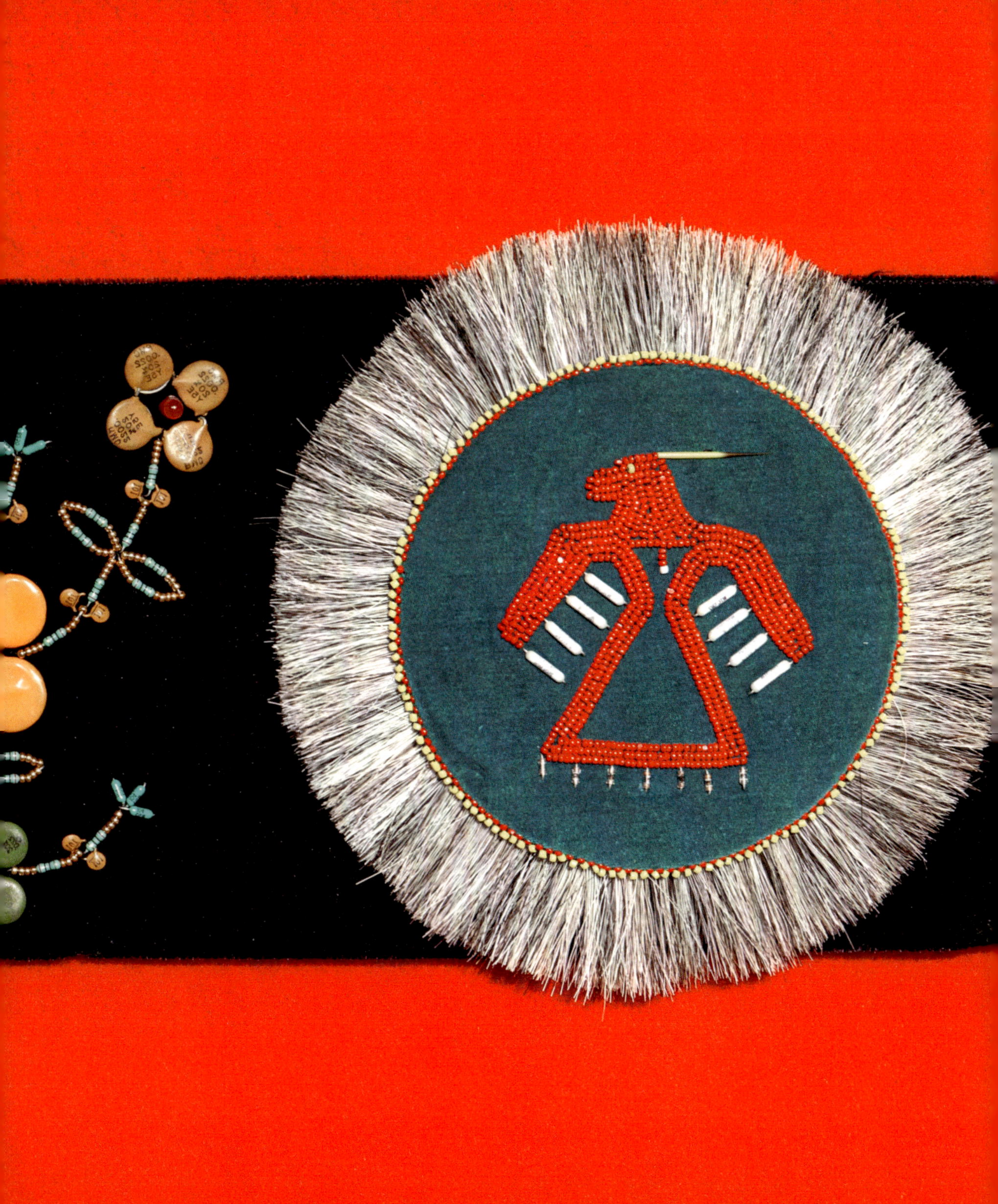

BREAKING THE MOLD

by Armand Garnet Ruffo

—

"I'm looking at those traditional arts and looking at how often the anthropological perspective puts our art in a historical stasis, and I like to challenge that.... Our culture has never been in a stasis."

—

BARRY ACE

ANISHINAABE-ODAWA VISUAL ARTIST,
POWWOW DANCER, CURATOR,
WRITER, AND ACTIVIST

Today the clouds are thick and hazy with meaning. Ziibi, a river. Inside them floats a story the birds hold in their hollow bones. Watch them reverberate and echo across time. A few years ago I found myself in the Montreal Museum of Fine Arts. I turned to view a painting, and I found myself in the Art Gallery of Ontario. It startled me, because I turned again and I was standing in the First Peoples gallery at the Royal Ontario Museum in Toronto. And again, and there I was at the Woodland Cultural Centre in Brantford. It is like that sometimes. I remember now. In Montreal I was looking at a portrait that is over one hundred years old. A painterly light caught a young man's dark face. Who was he? A sunrise flared behind him. Or was it a sunset? I wanted to know more about the painting, and I took up my phone and with the swipe of my hand the past came into view. Again, I looked closely at him, and I saw that his gaze was fixed upwards into the far distance. What was he observing? Ziibi, a river? It was then that I realized, just as for me he was the past, where I stood I was the future.

———

It begins with a common enough occurrence. The year is 1838, and a handsome twenty-three-year-old Huron-Wendat, known by his people as Telariolin, by the French as Zacharie Vincent, is asked to sit for his portrait. Dressed in a stylish white waistcoat highlighted by a red sash and a silver brooch, the young man travels fifteen kilometres south to Quebec City from his village of Jeune-Lorette/Wendake, where nearly two centuries earlier his displaced ancestors sought refuge with the Jesuits. There he enters the studio of French-Canadian artist Antoine Plamondon who during a pause in the painting lets Vincent casually pick up a tiny brush. In the course of a few days he instructs him how to hold it properly, the tip of his thumb and forefinger applying the right amount of pressure, how to dip it into a pot of paint, how to touch and stroke the canvas ever so delicately. Vincent realizes this is something he can do, and he sets about making a likeness of his own hand. Lower Canada, and a Huron-Wendat is making art in the Western mode. It is a moment of art history.

Plamondon is surprised to see such potential in Vincent's foray into portraiture. He encourages the burgeoning young artist each time he visits, and over a pipe of tobacco he lends his advice. Vincent is given tips on Western pictorial techniques such as perspective, light, and colour, and perhaps even more importantly what this idea of making art is all about. It is during these visits that he decides to become an artist. Here we see a butterfly slowly emerging from his diaphanous chrysalis into beauty. He will go on to paint six hundred paintings in his lifetime, selling them to visiting high-ranking English dignitaries such as Lord Durham and Lord Elgin, as well as officials, soldiers, tourists, and patrons. And yet there is something guarded behind the surface of Telariolin's interest. He will take it upon himself to learn everything he can about painting from Plamondon and others like the renowned Cornelius Krieghoff, his goal to control his own image and those of his people, refute the depictions of Western stereotypes, the exotic and tragic backward-looking savage.

———

Herein is the second entry of our observation. It is of another life that echoes and circles a similar and familiar pattern. It is that of George Henry, known as Maungwudaus by his Credit River Mississauga-Ojibwe people. Now it is 1845, and the Mississauga who are living on the shores and inland of Lake Ontario have been coerced into a series of treaties that have all but dispossessed them of their lands. What little is left is constantly invaded by settlers who will not move despite the King's assurances. "As it is, the poor Indian seems hardly destined to meet *justice*, either from the legislative or executive power,"[1] writes Anna Brownell Jameson, an observer of the time. An intelligent, capable boy, Maungwudaus has had a Western education through the Methodist Mission in Upper Canada, becoming a translator and missionary, and, as Reverend William Case describes him, "a tolerable poet." Disillusioned by both church and government, he reclaims his Mississauga identity and sets sail for Europe. With a dance troupe assembled from family members and friends, he embarks on a three-year voyage. The purpose of Maungwudaus's journey is multifarious, but it is clear that he seeks out the powerful King Louis Philippe of France, and Sir Augustus d'Este and Dr. Thomas Hodgkin, members of the Aboriginal Protection Society in England. A stolen person in a foreign land, Henry sets out to the heart of those nations that have done the stealing.

There is yet another side to Henry that rests in his interest in poetry and art. Among those he meets in England are the American painter and author George Catlin, celebrated as the first white man to travel the western plains and paint Native Americans in their own territory. They become friends and business partners. In the busy opulence of the Egyptian Hall in London and the Salle Valentino in Paris, Catlin displays his elaborately decorated Pawnee and Mandan likenesses. In the backdrop of hundreds of embellished "Indian paintings," Maungwudaus and his dance troupe perform a "tableau vivant" in full regalia to bring life to the art. The spectacle inspires other artists. In Paris he becomes acquainted with one of France's greatest Romantic painters, Eugène Delacroix, who sketches his likeness. In Scotland he visits the cottage of the famed Robbie Burns, the national poet. And while in England he makes a point of traveling to Stratford-upon-Avon to visit the grave of William Shakespeare. Activist, dancer, performer, entrepreneur, and poet, he proudly plays with the construction of the exotic Indian, making sure to sign the registry in his Anishinaabe name, Maungwudaus, the Hero.

It is about this time that traders introduce silk, velvet, ribbons, glass seed beads, and thread into Indigenous communities. The new technology is readily adopted by the Ojibwe in the mid to late 1800s and incorporated into their clothing. Dresses and shirts of arresting power and beauty are stitched with precision. Intricately beaded designs depict a pantheon of Manitou spirits and realistic representation of local flora and fauna. Binesi/Thunderbird, Makwa/Bear, Waezauwaubugooneek/ Buttercup: this is the type of regalia that Maungwudaus and his compatriots wear as they travel Europe, drawing crowds of thousands in their wake. Freedom, however, is short-lived. By the early 1900s, Canada's Indian policy is one of ruthless assimilation. "A weird and waning race"[2] is the descriptor Duncan Campbell Scott, Deputy Superintendent of the Department of Indian Affairs, uses at the time.

Without a substantial land base, local Indigenous economies are in ruins and the people struggle. They turn to their traditions, and do what they have done for centuries, adapt them to the circumstances of the time. Witness: one hundred years later a touring exhibition of Indigenous objects from the nineteenth century made for tourists; split ash letter holders, beaded pincushions and doilies, moose hair tufted bags, birchbark coasters, miniature canoes, and paddles. Traditional artistic practice reinvented, innovated.

———

A third entry to our observations resides deeper in the idea of reconstructing oneself through one's art. In the light of a gallery, we move from Telariolin Zacharie Vincent and Maungwudaus George Henry to Tekahionwake E. Pauline Johnson, renowned nineteenth century Mohawk poet and performer who challenged the establishment of the time, drawing devoted crowds to her recitals. Born on Six Nations reserve and laid to rest in Vancouver, she ascends through the dawn in a city that holds its largest public funeral ever. Flags at half-mast, offices closed, crowds lining the streets, horse-drawn carriages, the Squamish people in solemn procession. A hundred years later we still search to understand who she really was. Yesterday—or was it a year ago?—I went for walk and found myself in the Agnes Etherington Art Centre in Kingston, standing in front of her two stage dresses: a typical white Victorian gown and her own self-assembled "Red Indian" dress. E. Pauline Johnson and Tekahionwake—her grandmother's name and her adopted stage name, the myth of her like a tangled garden tugged at my ankles.

> *A cordon of wire and over 100 years separates us my dear Pauline,*
> *and there you are staring me down in that same dress arms bare,*
> *hands on hips, head tilted back eyes flipping time. And here we are*
> *still trying to respond in the only way we know how.*[3]

A single, poor, Indian woman who learns to fend for herself and not only survives but with ambition and resolve thrives in a literary world dominated by white men. Daring, audacious, her performances challenge genres, her own body becomes her art. Lace-trimmed, modest white gown, a fur stole, in sharp contrast to a buckskin dress, bear claw necklace, red sash, feather fan held high in a salute to creation. Pauline chanting, reciting, singing her poetry in high drama. Her Victorian audiences charmed by her Christian civility, scandalized, titillated, by her Heathen savagery. Tekahionwake, a life performed, the consummate performance artist—a term that does not exist in her time (and there's that word again, time)—and therein the gallery begins to disappear. Tekahionwake, poet trailblazer, angry historian, proud Canadian, lonely and uncertain mixed-blood woman, leading the way for countless other women, moving further and further into her art.

———

There is an old black-and-white CBC film from the 1960s featuring the great Ojibwe painter Norval Morrisseau that held me in its grasp long before I decided to write about him. As the film spins out its images, time stops, and there is the young Morrisseau, tall, thin, wearing rubber boots on a hot summer day. I first saw his art in the late 1970s, and I was awestruck, but it was the image of him in his ramshackle house in Beardmore with a tree literally growing through the roof that really made me want to know more about him. What became clear as spring water was that the key to understanding his groundbreaking art was to understand his Anishinaabe worldview, and it sent me on a journey that lasted for years. I realized that it is a belief system so far outside of Western philosophical tradition that it was unrecognizable to the newcomers who quickly dismissed it as primitive and without purpose or worth. Their impassive response was to set about cutting down the trees, first to build their homes, and then for economic exploitation. "A Canadian settler *hates* a tree, regards it as his natural enemy, as something to be destroyed, eradicated, annihilated by all and any means,"[4] wrote Jameson in 1838 on touring Upper Canada. We are still living with the consequences.

If we are the past, then we are fed on the mother's milk of history. On Ziibi, a river of time. From 1815 to 1850, a short period of thirty-five years, one million immigrants hungry for land swarm the Canadas by the shiploads. "The stench of packed humanity creeps ahead on the breeze to warn of their impending arrival."[5] They disembark sick with cholera and smallpox which devastates Indigenous populations. The arrivals never cease. Picture roads of mud, fields of barren stumps, lumber camps, shantytowns, where once stood a spectacular forest of red oak, white pine, beech, birch, and spruce. If we listen hard enough we can still hear trees the height of cathedrals crashing down around us, feel the heat of the fires, the smell of the smoke. It is our world coming down around us. Picture a people witnessing the end of it, carrying their young and old, sick and dying. They pray that some may live. Pray for the newborn. Pray for the unborn. For those who now live a life they could never have fathomed in all their dreaming.

If we are the present. "My people, be proud of your great culture,"[6] writes Morrisseau. Water, Nibi. Land, Aki. Life, Bimaadiziwin. A "Memory Landscape."[7] In the 1990s Odawa artist Barry Ace was Chief Curator of the Indian Art Centre at the Department of Indian and Northern Affairs[8]. I spoke often to him about Norval Morrisseau at the time, and later when I began writing my books about Morrisseau. Separated by a generation, their art practices are ostensibly very different, and yet there is a common thread woven like one of Ace's intricate bandoliers. Look for it. In the old traditions. In the sacred places where we still lay down tobacco to honour the spirits of the four directions, the seven stages of life. Where our ancestors dance with us through time. Where their presence rises to the surface of dream, an inland sea, and Misshipeshu, water spirit, swims below and pulls us under. That is us in the gallery searching for connection. We all want so badly to be whole. We lean into each other as we have always done. We lean into the image makers as we have always done. And realize that today the intricately patterned beads are computer parts, capacitors, resistors, discarded waste, the detritus of our age. A contemporary inheritance.

If we are the future. The birds speak—as does all life—they circle overhead and tell us that Western science is finally catching up. It now verifies that the belief in the primacy of a holistic connection to Mother Earth holds important truths for humanity. It is an ancient body of knowledge about the natural world that Indigenous people draw upon to find connection to all living things, and in so doing find our place in the world. Balance and belonging are primary states of being passed from one generation to the next, and they are integral to Indigenous modes of expression. A song carried by a drum. A story told in a sweat lodge.

An image painted on a rock face. "Bound together / transformed / innumerable times / by innumerable artists / so that the people might continue."[9] It is no longer acceptable to clear cut the trees as far as the eye can see. It will become unacceptable to create *things* without understanding that they too have a life cycle. They too will eventually return to the earth, to their component parts.

———

Look, over there sits a dark-haired Anishinaabe hard at work. Transformed by place and time, he holds a gleaming needle in his hand. His head is bent in concentration. His movements are gentle and precise. He looks up for a moment and smiles.

Armand Garnet Ruffo was born in Chapleau, northern Ontario, and draws on his Ojibwe heritage for his writing. He is the recipient of the 2020 Latner Writers' Trust Poetry Prize. His publications include *Norval Morrisseau: Man Changing Into Thunderbird* (2014) and *Treaty #* (2019), both finalists for Governor General's Literary Awards. His latest projects are the libretto for a musical drama, *Sounding Thunder: The Song of Francis Pegahmagabow*, and a collaborative film, *"On The Day The World Begins Again,"* a video-poem about the incarceration of Indigenous peoples. Ruffo's poetry most recently appeared in *The Best Canadian Poetry in English 2020* (Tightrope Books). He teaches at Queen's University in Kingston, Ontario.

1 Anna Brownell Jameson, *Winter Studies and Summer Rambles in Canada*. Reprint. Toronto: McClelland & Stewart, 1990.

2 Duncan Campbell Scott, "The Onondaga Madonna,"*CanLit Guides, Canadian Literature* "The Onondaga Madonna." *CanLit Guides, Canadian Literature*. Vancouver: University of British Columbia, 8 Aug 2012. http://canlitguides.ca/canlit-guides-editorial-team/poetry-and-racialization/the-onondaga-madonna-1898-by-duncan-campbell-scott-and-racialization/

3 Armand Garnet Ruffo, "Pauline Johnson's Dress, 1892," *Treaty #*. Hamilton, ON: Wolsak & Wynn, 2019.

4 Jameson, *Winter Studies and Summer Rambles in Canada*.

5 Eric Ross, *Full of Hope and Promise, the Canadas in 1841*. Kingston, ON: McGill-Queen's University Press, 1991.

6 Norval Morrisseau, *Legends of My People, the Great Ojibway*, ed. Selwyn Dewdney. Toronto: McGraw-Hill Ryerson, 1965.

7 Barry Ace, "Memory Landscape." Digital output on archival canvas, glass beads, wood, hide. 33" x 81". Collection of the artist, 2014.

8 Now the Indigenous Art Centre, Crown–Indigenous Relations and Northern Affairs Canada (CIRNAC).

9 Armand Garnet Ruffo, "Indian Canoe," *The Thunderbird Poems*. Madeira Park, BC: Harbour Publishing, 2015.

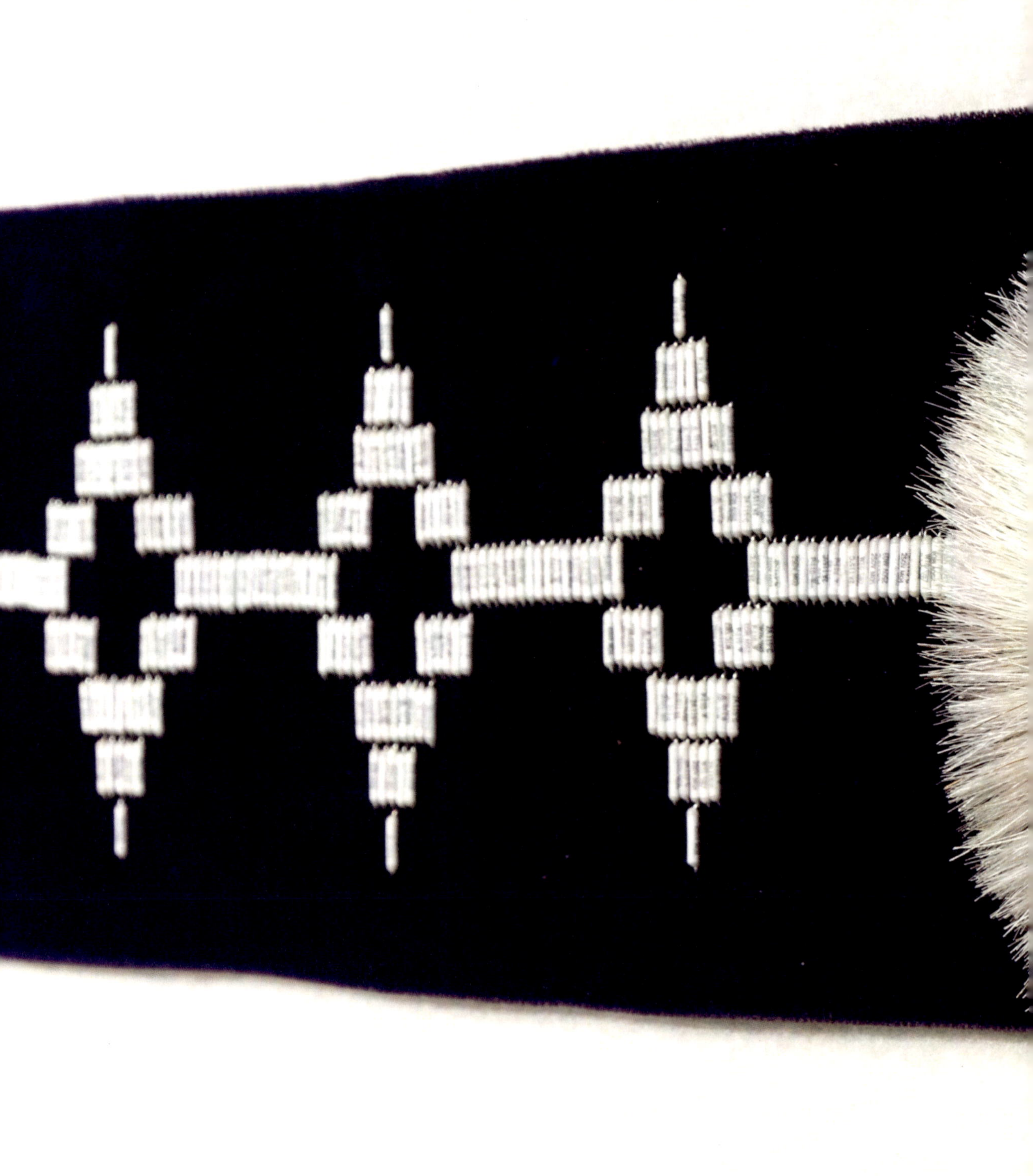

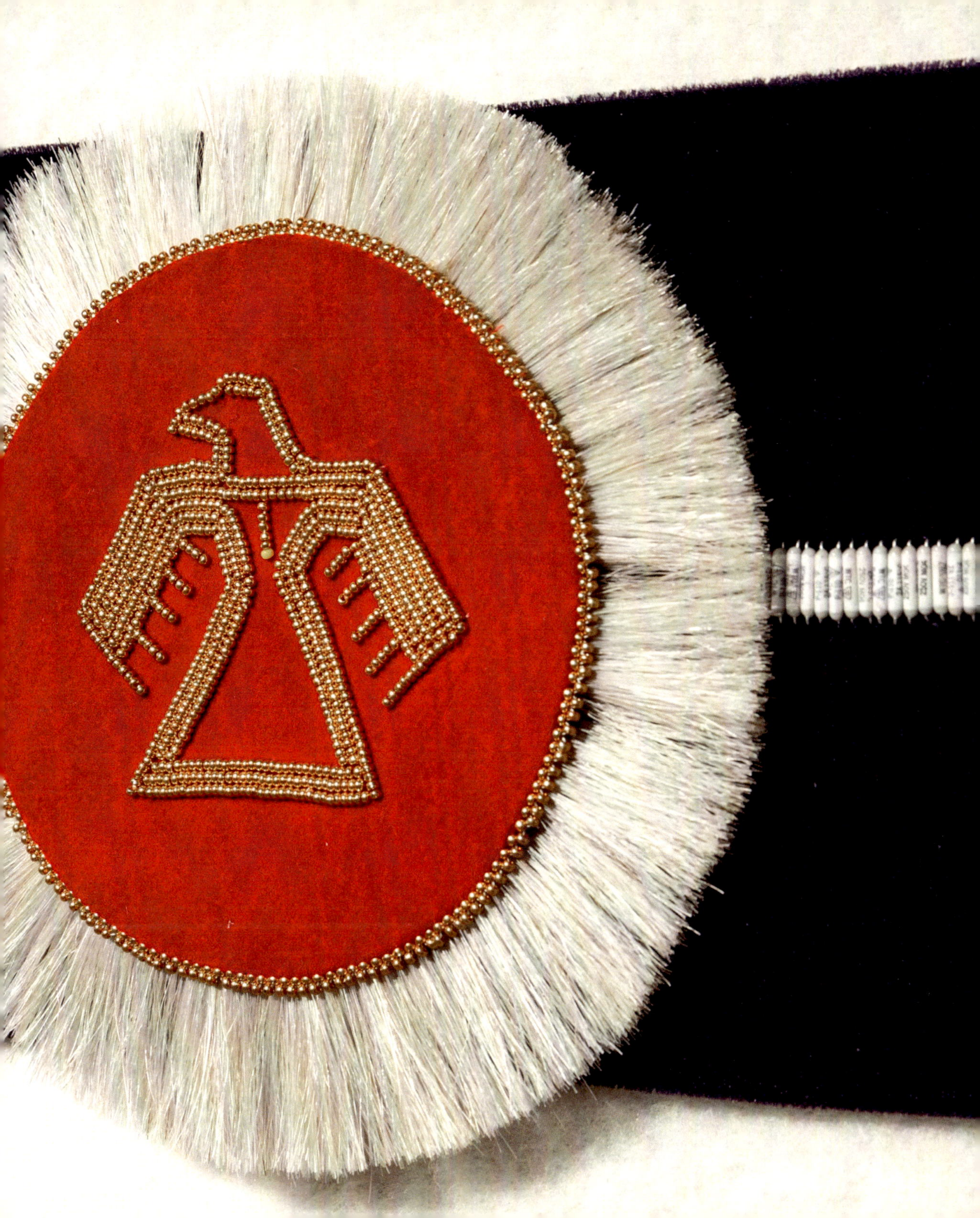

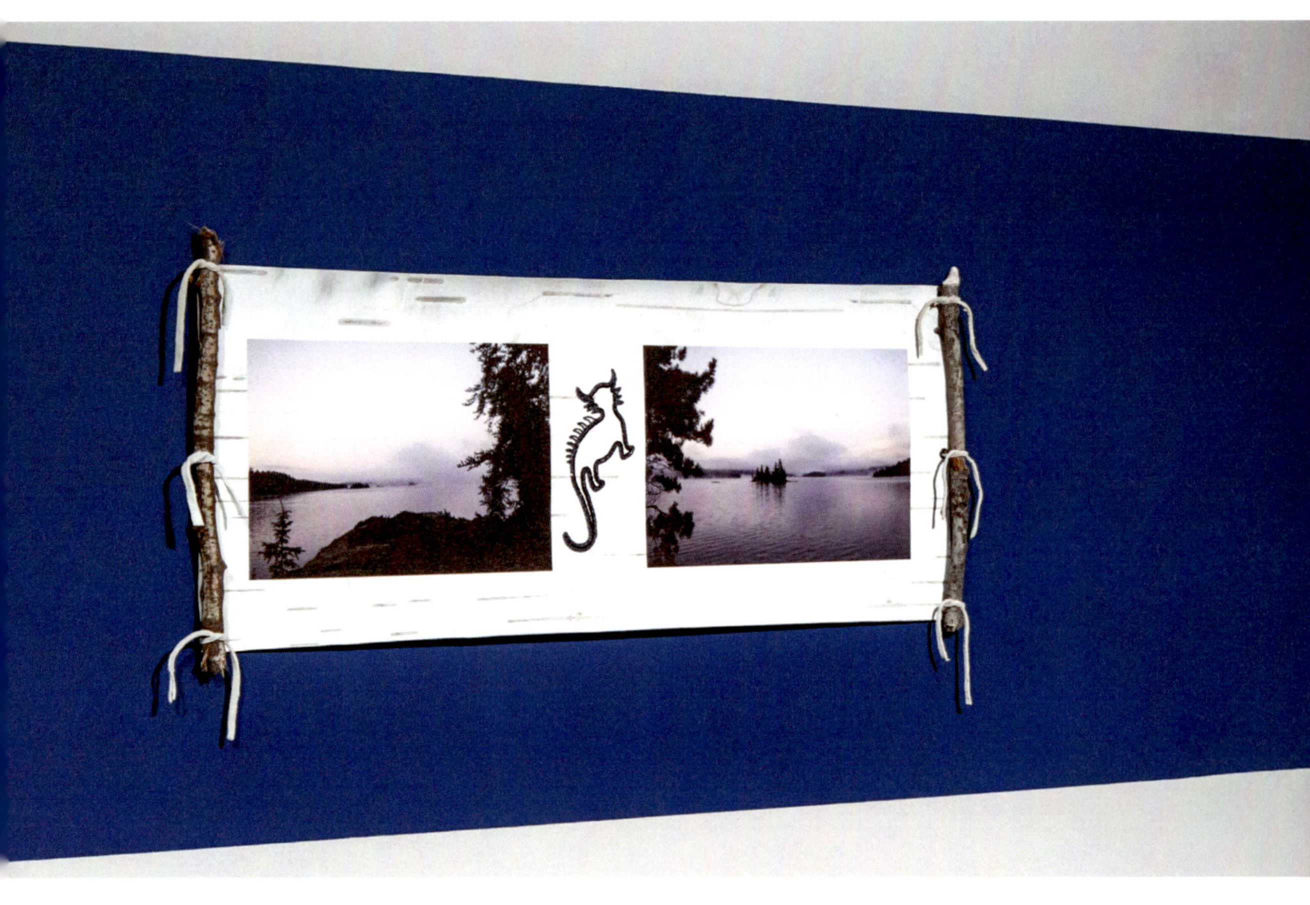

Aanikegamaa-gichigami: Lake Erie (Chain of Lakes Sea),
Detail, 2016, Hudson Bay blanket, velvet, beads, electronic
components, metal, mountain climbing rope.

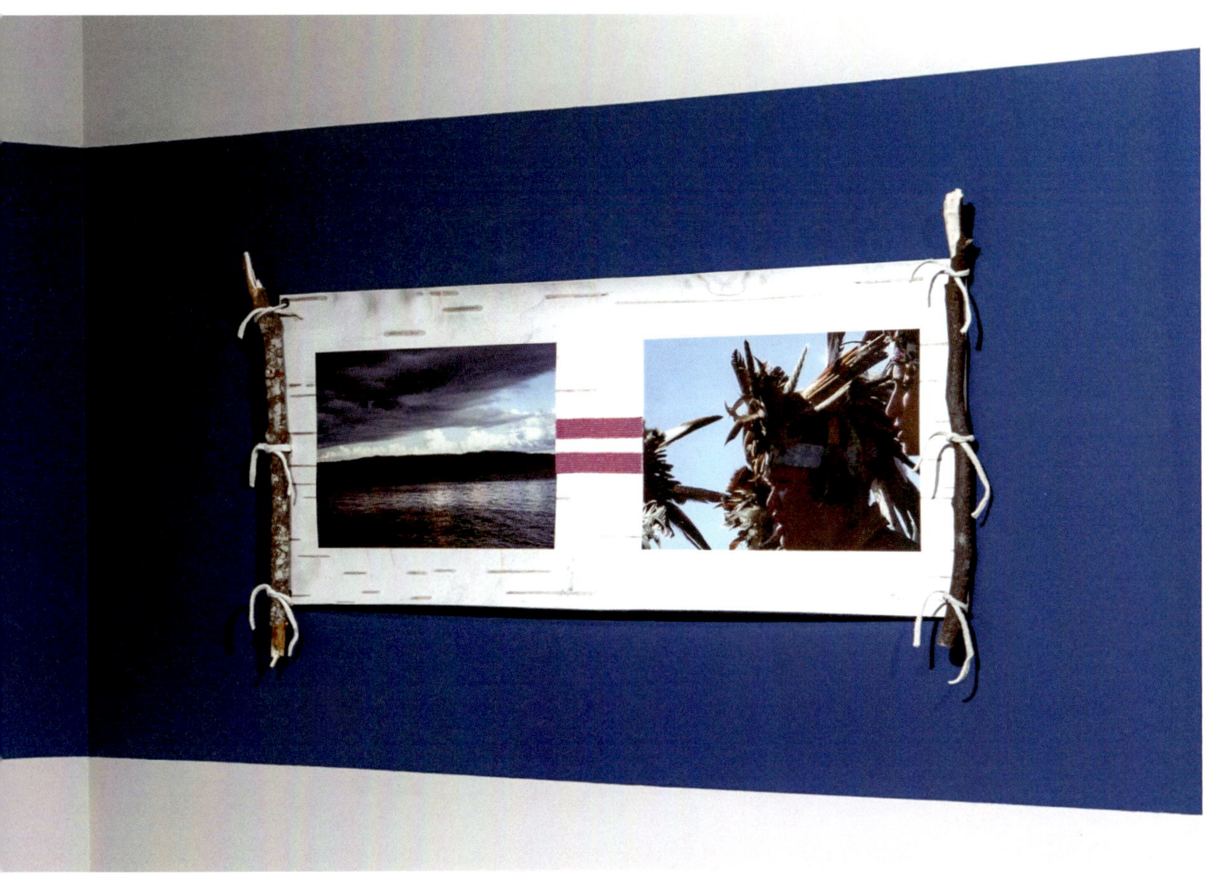

Memory Landscape, (select précis of 30), Detail, 2014,
Digital output on archival canvas, glass beads, wood, hide.

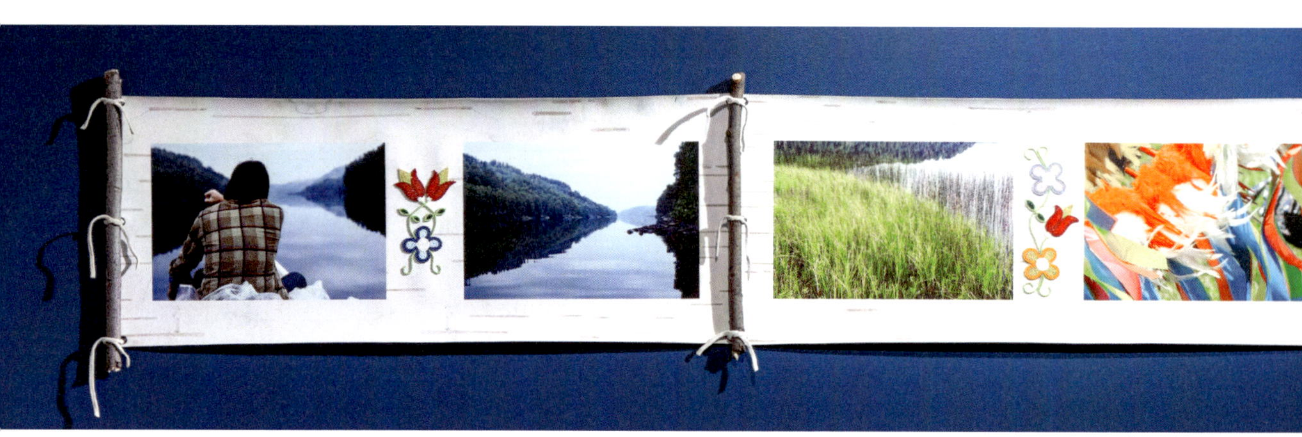

Memory Landscape, (select précis of 30), 2014,
Digital output on archival canvas, glass beads, wood, hide.

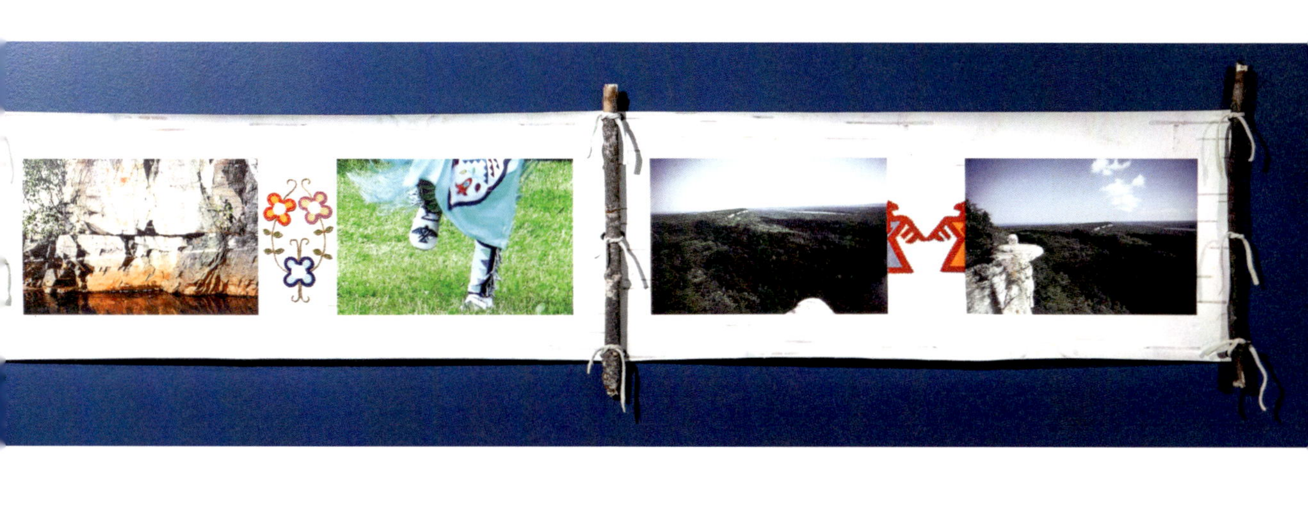

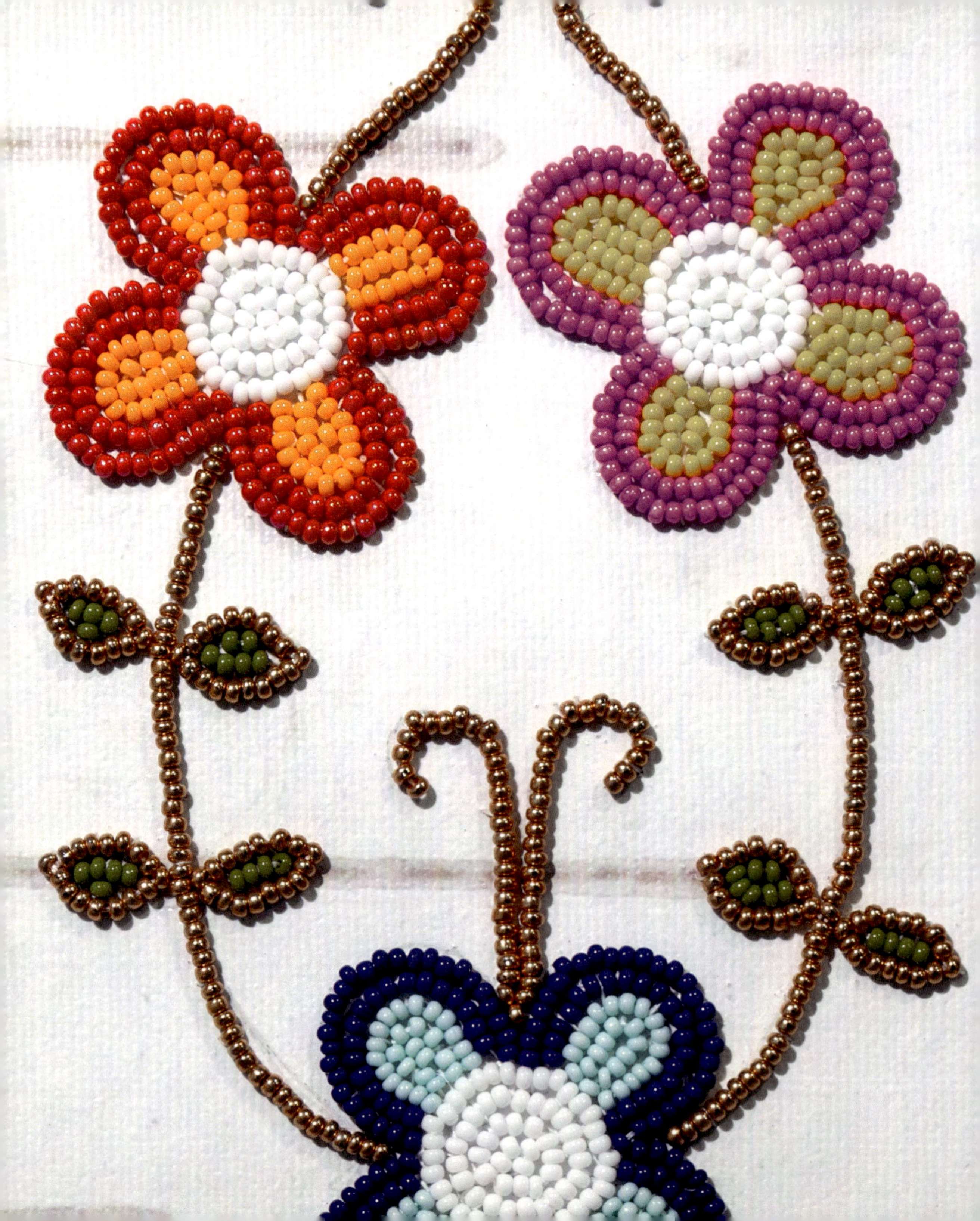

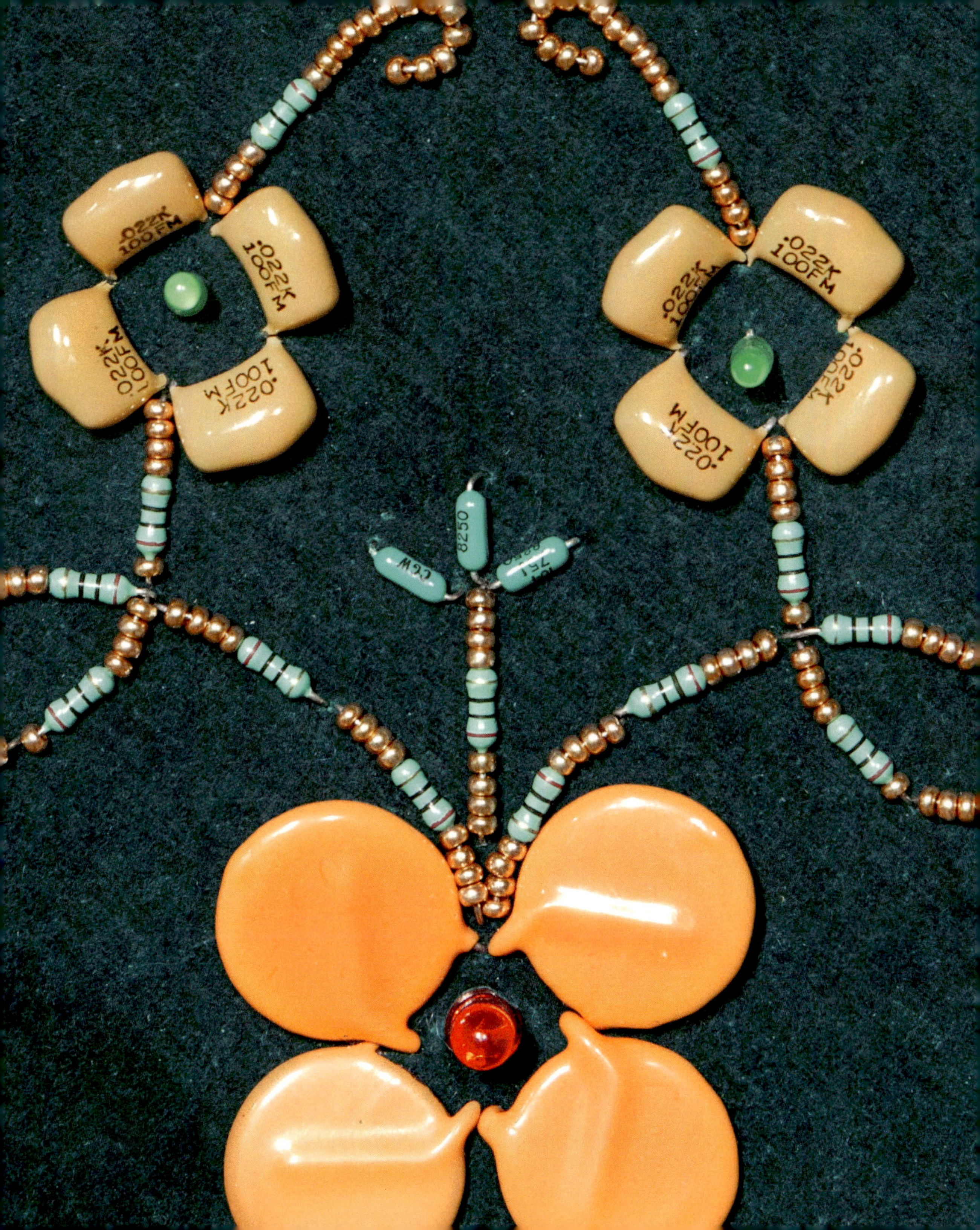

.022K
100FM
.022K
100FM
.022K
100FM
.022K
100FM
.022K
100FM
.022K
100FM
.022K
100FM
.022K
100FM
8250

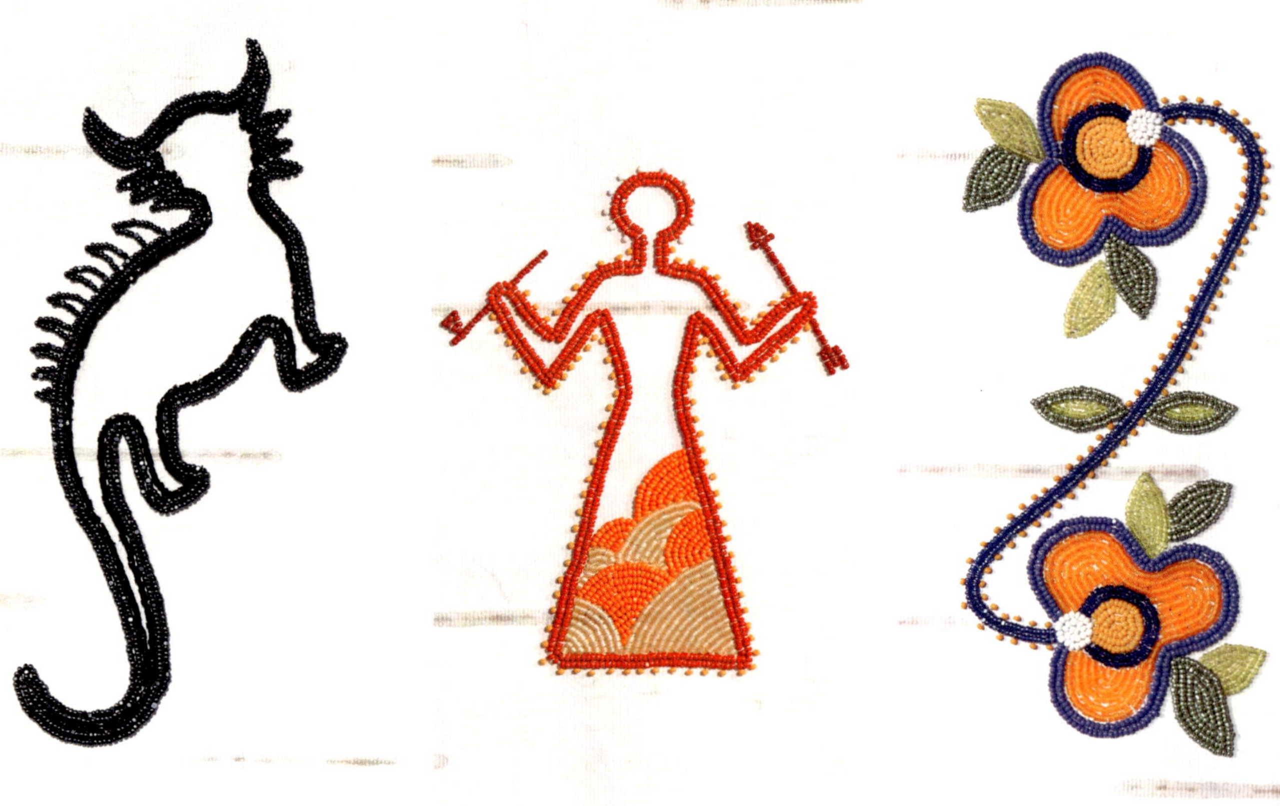

Memory Landscape, (select précis of 30), Details, 2014,
Digital output on archival canvas, glass beads, wood, hide.

Memory Landscape, (select précis of 30), Details, 2014,
Digital output on archival canvas, glass beads, wood, hide.

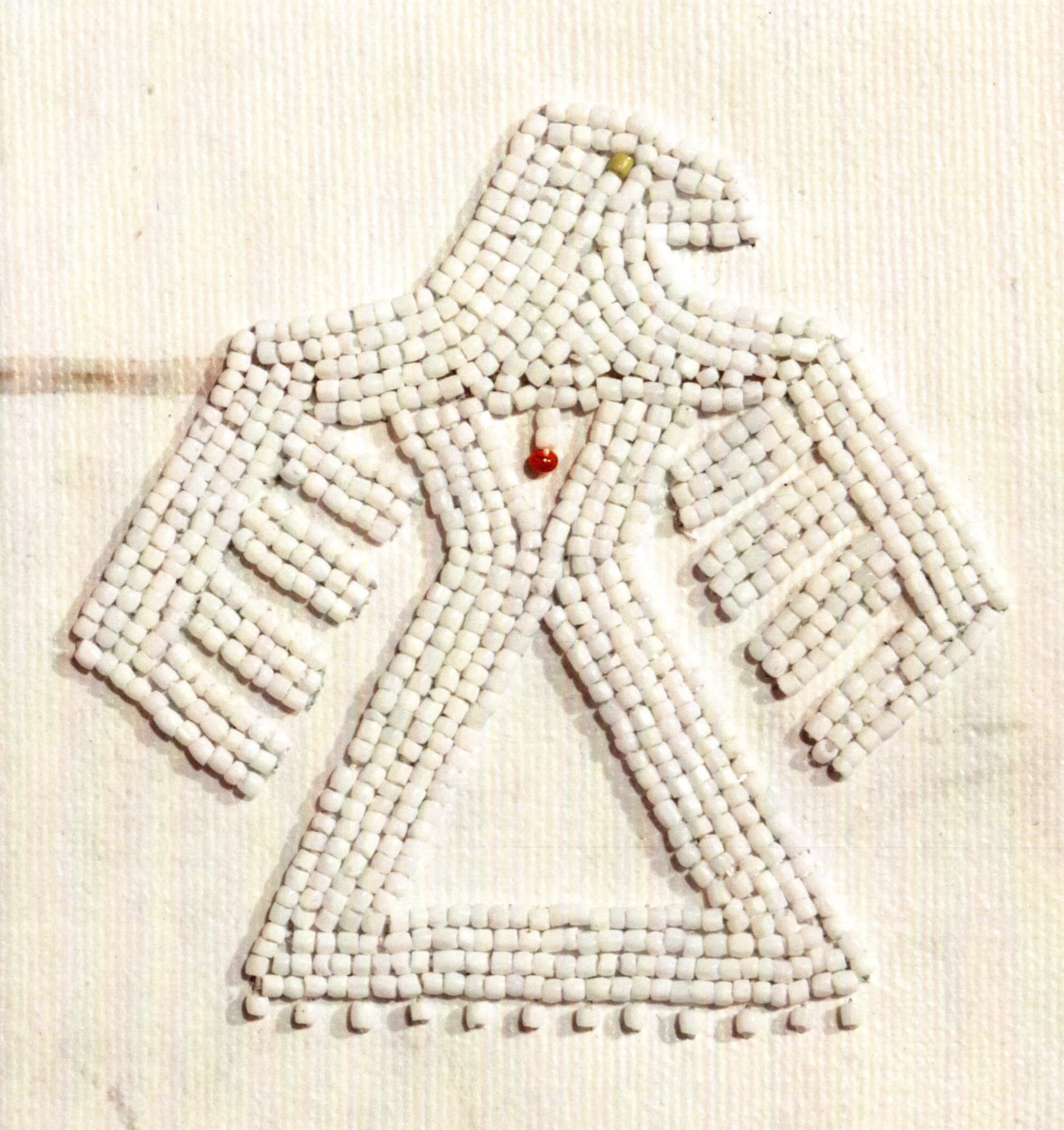

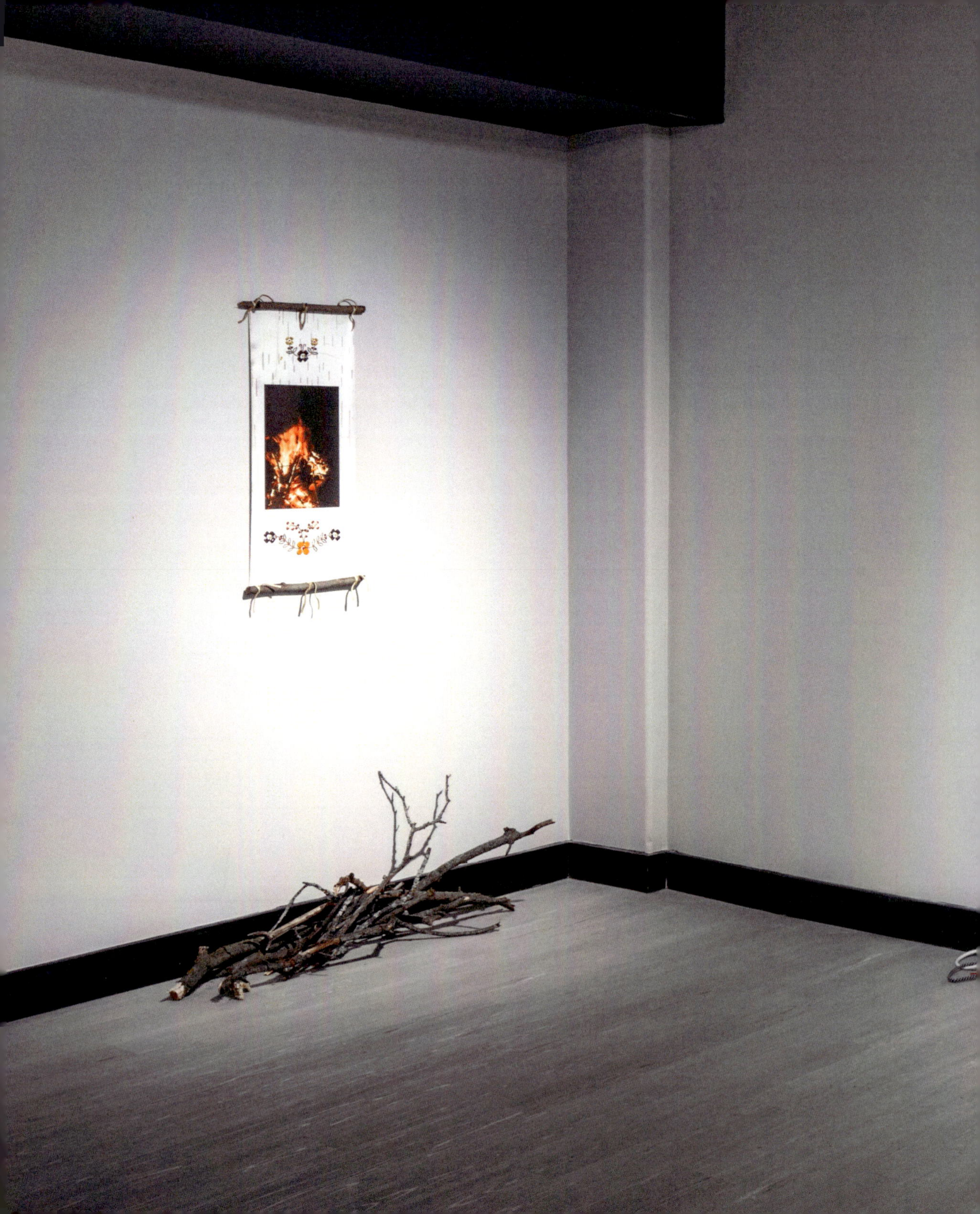

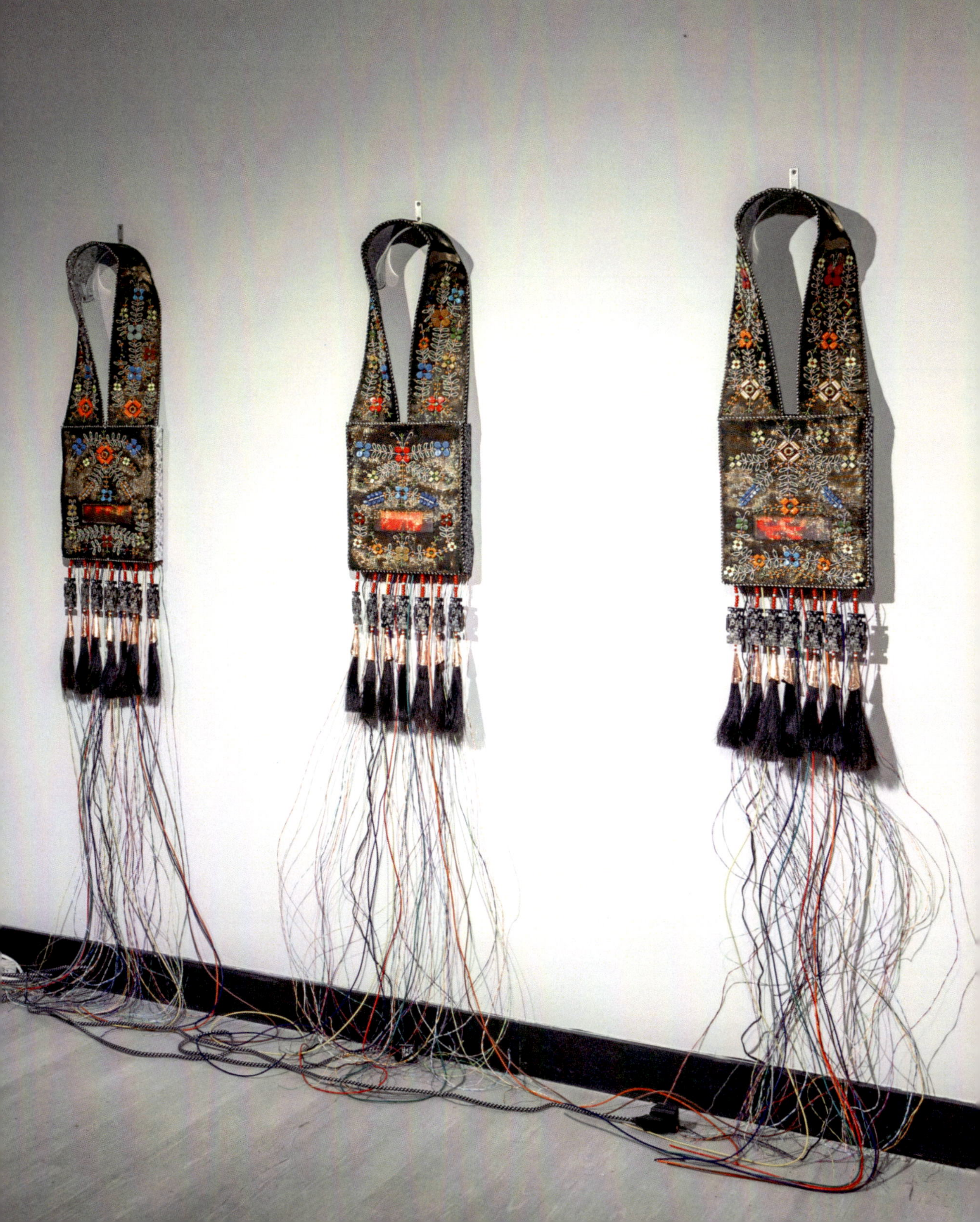

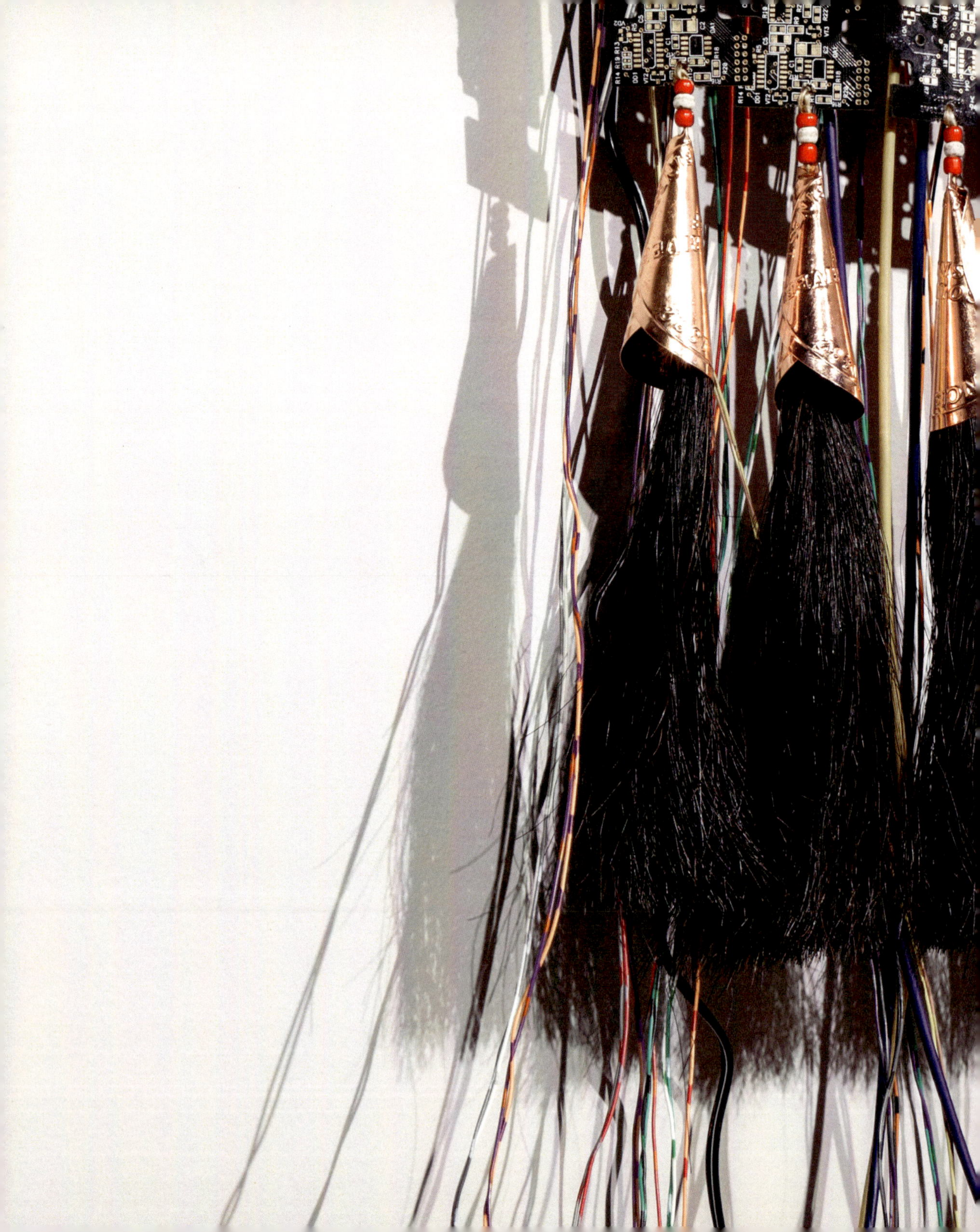

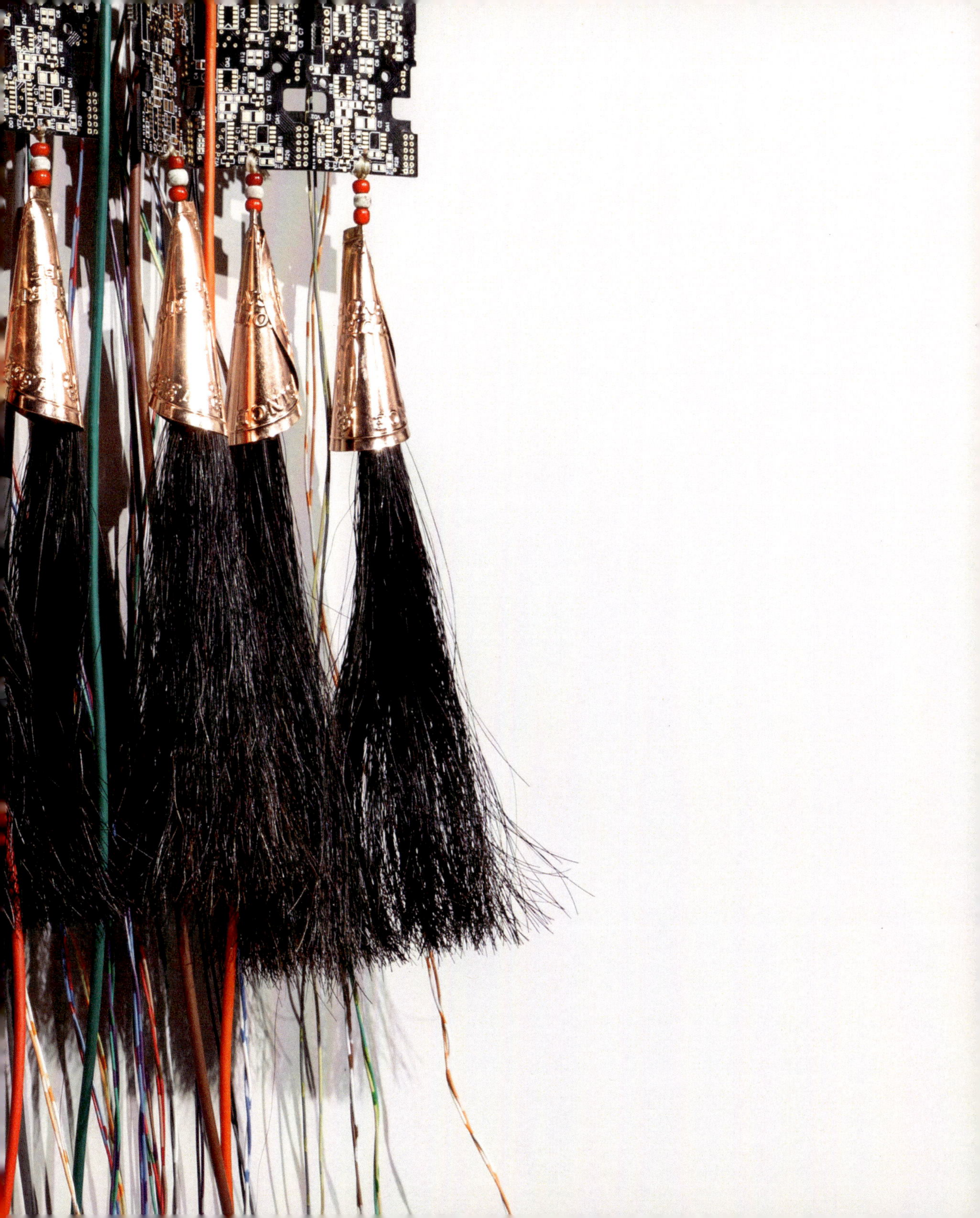

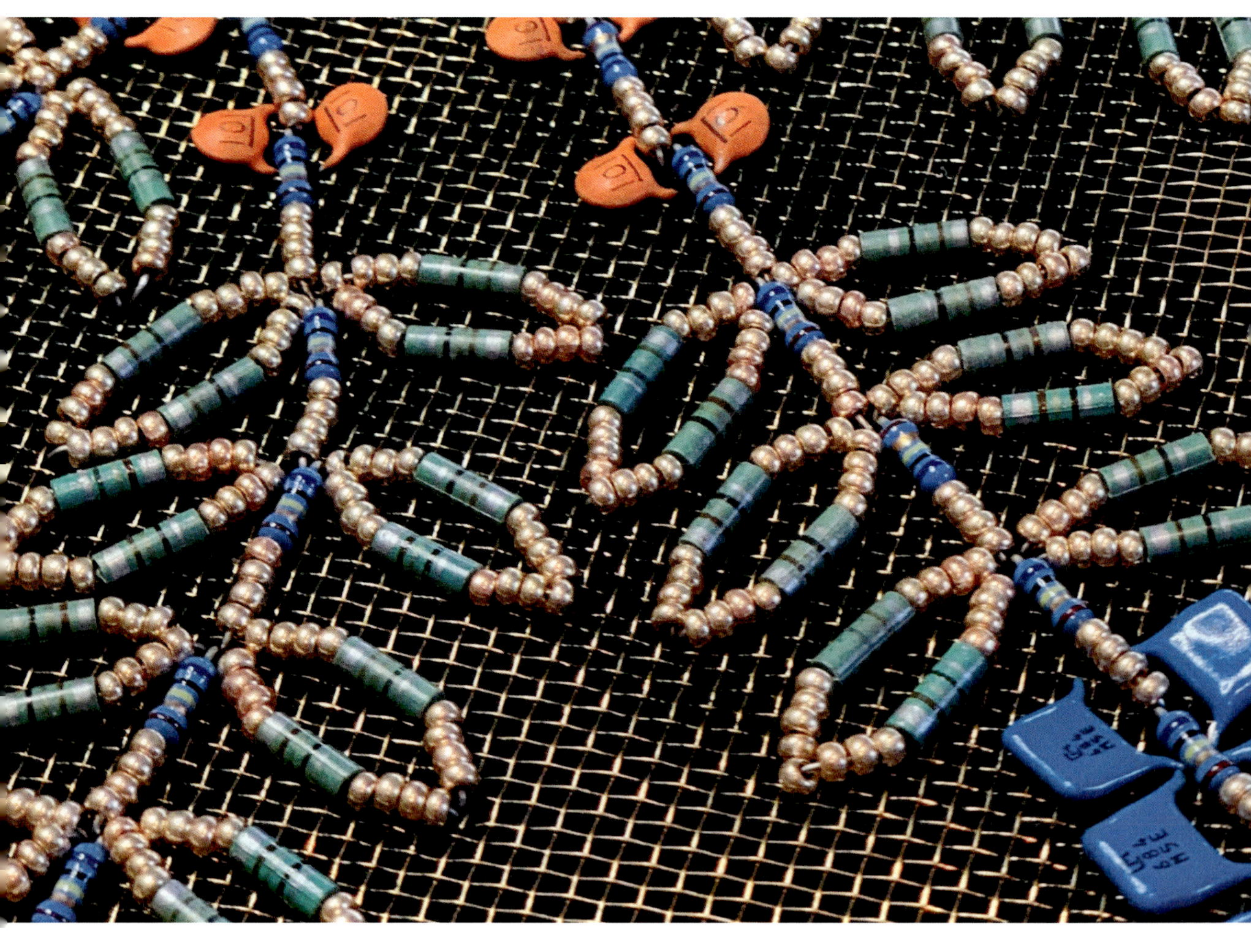

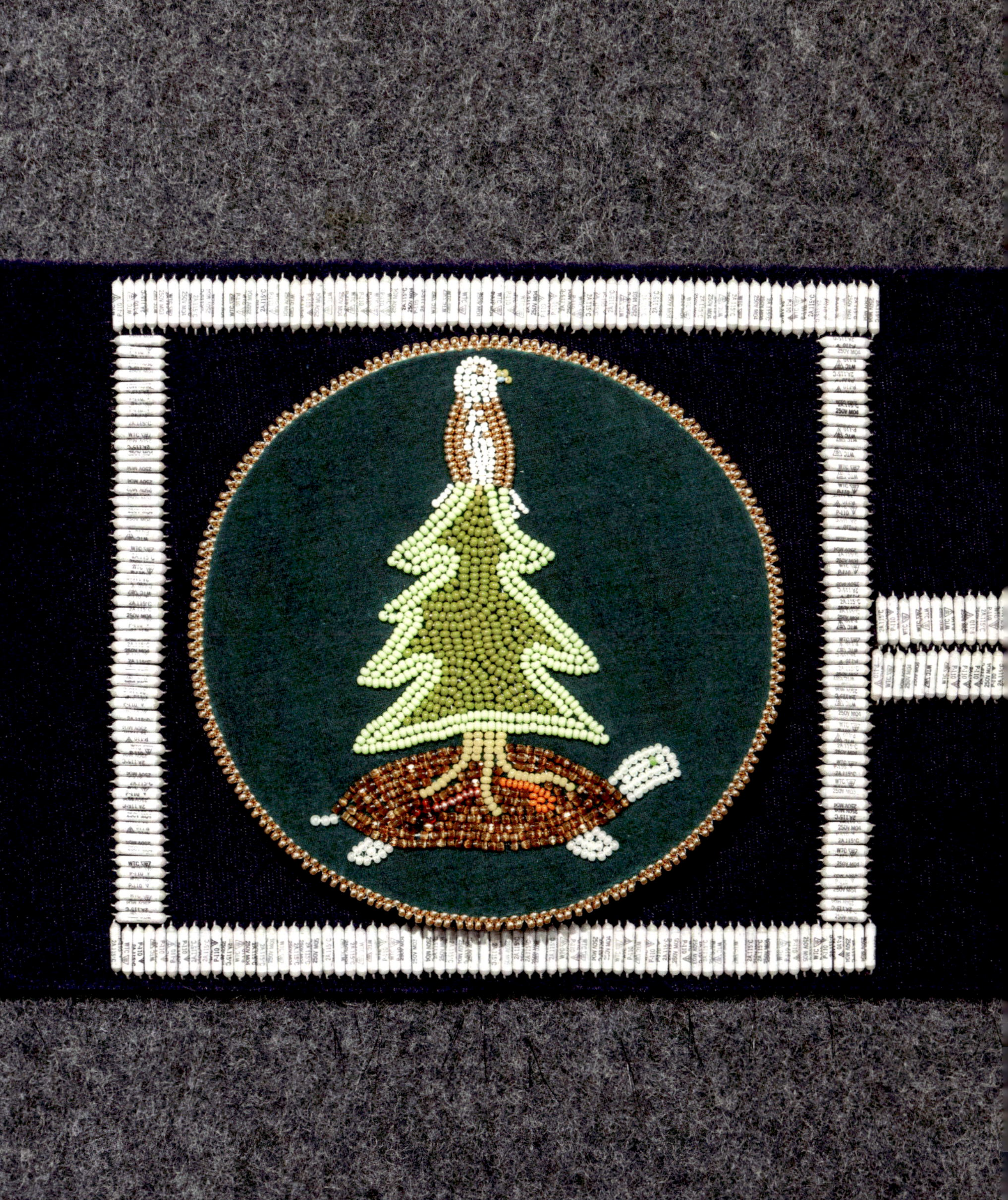

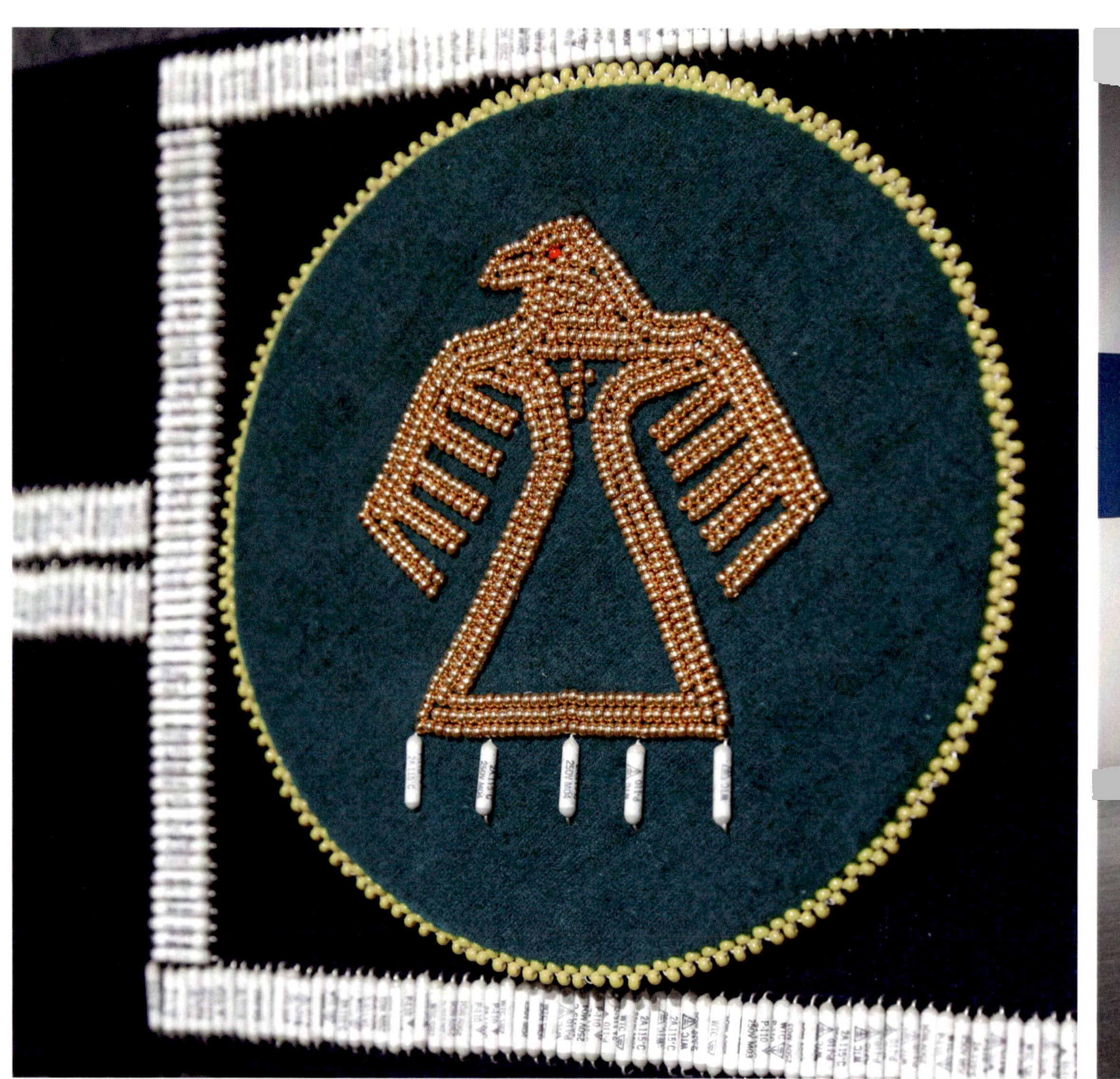

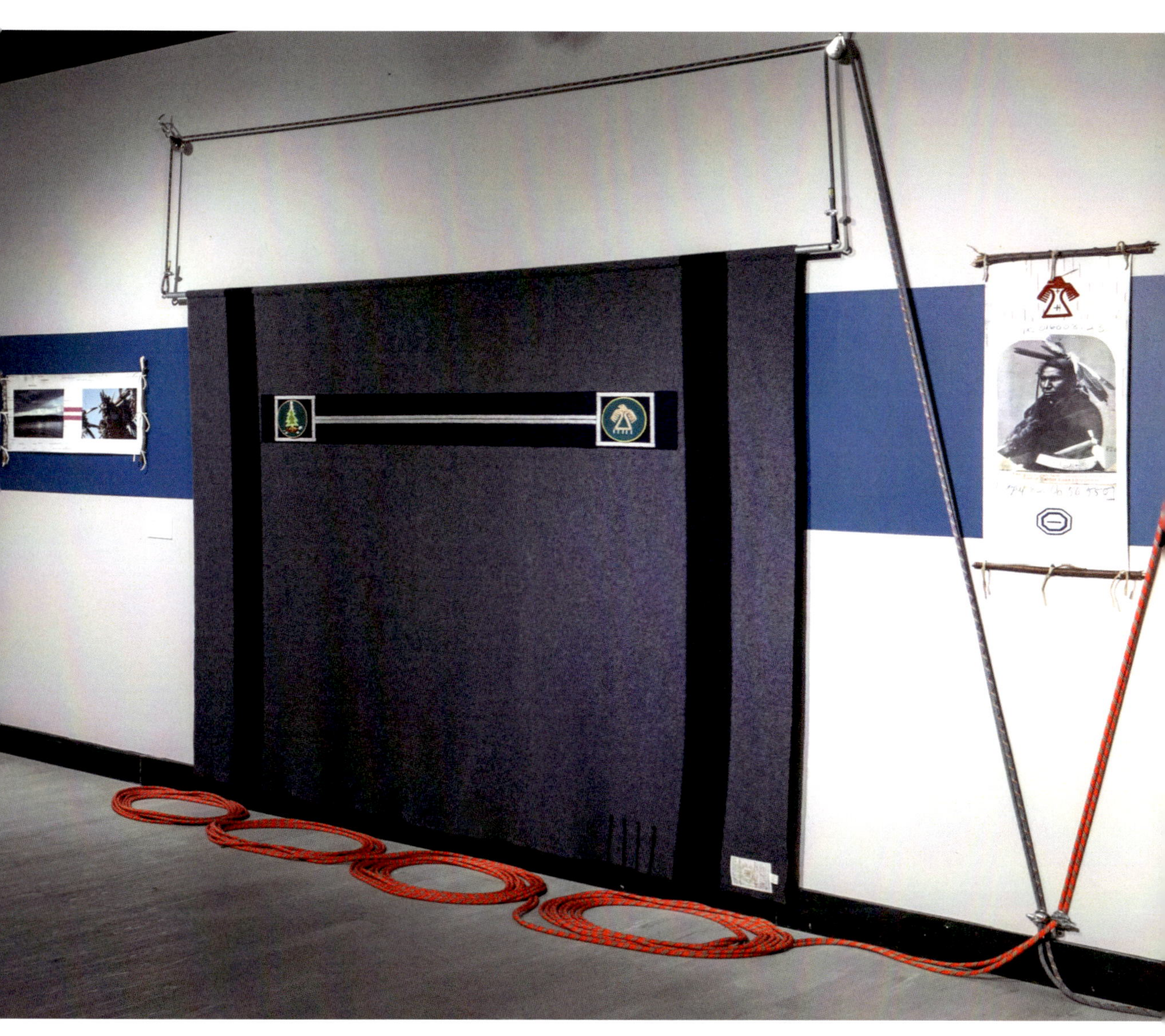

Barry Ace is a practising visual artist and a *debendaagzijig* (citizen) of M'Chigeeng First Nation, Odawa Mnis (Manitoulin Island), Ontario, Canada. His mixed media paintings and assemblage textile works explore various aspects of cultural continuity and the confluence of the historical and contemporary. Ace states that "as our digital age exponentially transforms and infuses Anishinaabeg culture (and other global cultures) with new technologies and new ways of communicating, we are harnessing and bridging the precipice between historical and contemporary knowledge, art, and power, while maintaining a distinct Anishinaabeg aesthetic connecting generations."

His work can be found in numerous public and private collections in Canada and abroad, including the *National Gallery of Canada* (Ottawa); *Canadian Museum of History* (Gatineau); *Art Gallery of Ontario* (Toronto); *Royal Ontario Museum* (Toronto); *Government of Ontario Art Collection* (Toronto); *City of Ottawa*; *Ottawa Art Gallery*; *Woodland Cultural Centre* (Brantford); *Canada Council Art Bank* (Ottawa); *North American Native Museum* (Zurich); *Ojibwe Cultural Foundation* (M'Chigeeng, Ontario); Global Affairs Canada (Ottawa); *TD Bank Art Collection* (Toronto); *Crown-Indigenous Relations and Northern Affairs Canada* (Gatineau); and *Westerkirk Works of Art* (Toronto).

In 2015, Barry was the recipient of the K. M. Hunter Artist Award for Visual Arts, administered by the Ontario Arts Council. He currently resides in Ottawa.

SELECTED EXHIBITIONS

- *Emergence from the Shadows—First Peoples Photographic Perspectives,* Canadian Museum of History, Gatineau, 1999.

- *Urban Myths: Aboriginal Artists in the City,* Karsh-Masson Gallery, Ottawa, 2000.

- *The Dress Show,* Leonard and Ellen Bina Art Gallery, Montreal, 2003.

- *Super Phat Nish,* Art Gallery of Southwestern Manitoba, Brandon, 2006.

- *50 Years of Pow wow,* Castle Gallery, New Rochelle, 2006.

- *Playing Tricks,* American Indian Community House Gallery, New York City, 2006.

- *"mðntu'c – little spirits, little powers,"* Nordamerika Native Museum, Zurich, 2010.

- *Changing Hands 3—Art Without Reservations,* Museum of Art and Design, New York City, 2012–2014.

- *Native Fashion Now: North American Native Style,* Peabody Essex Museum, Salem, 2016–2017.

- *Anishinaabeg Art and Power,* Royal Ontario Museum, Toronto, 2017.

- *Every. Now. Then. Reframing Nationhood,* Art Gallery of Ontario, Toronto, 2017.

- *2017 Canadian Biennial,* National Gallery of Canada, Ottawa, 2017.

- *We'll All Become Stories,* Ottawa Art Gallery, Ottawa, 2018.

- *URL : IRL,* Dunlop Art Gallery, Regina, 2018.

- *Public Disturbance: Politics and Protest in Contemporary Indigenous Art from Canada,* Supermarket 2018, Stockholm, 2018.

- *Coalesce,* Robert Langen Art Gallery, Waterloo, 2019.

- *Carbon and Light: Juan Geuer's Luminous Precision,* Ottawa Art Gallery, Ottawa, 2019.

- *Wrapped In Culture,* Ottawa Art Gallery, Ottawa, 2019.

- *Body of Waters,* Idea Exchange, Cambridge, 2019.

- *Abadakone,* National Gallery of Canada, Ottawa, 2019.

- *mazinigwaaso / to bead something,* Faculty of Fine Art Gallery Concordia University, Montreal, 2019.

Library and Archives Canada Cataloguing in Publication

Title: Coalesce.
Names: Ace, Barry, artist. | Ruffo, Armand Garnet, writer of added commentary. |
    Robert Langen Art Gallery, host institution, publisher.
Description: Text by Armand G. Ruffo. | Catalogue of an exhibition held at the
    Robert Langen Art Gallery from February 25 to April 5, 2019.
Identifiers: Canadiana 20200343769 | ISBN 9780994036131 (softcover)
Subjects: LCSH: Ace, Barry—Exhibitions. | LCGFT: Exhibition catalogs.
Classification: LCC N6549.A24 A4 2020 | DDC 709.2—dc23

Robert Langen Art Gallery
Wilfrid Laurier University
75 University Avenue West
Waterloo, ON N2L 3C3

Catalogue Acknolwedgements:
Suzanne Luke CURATOR
Armand Garnet Ruffo ESSAY
Murray Tong EDITOR
Scott Lee PHOTOGRAPHER
Betty Winge GRAPHIC DESIGNER
Marquis PRINTER
Robert Langen Art Gallery PUBLISHER

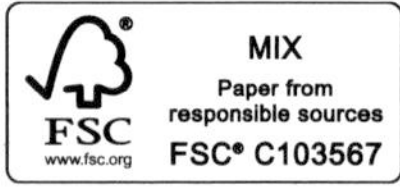

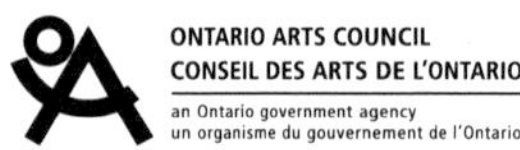

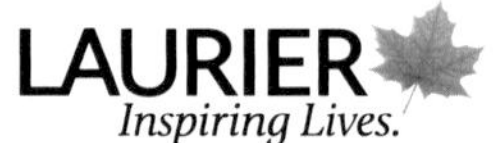